Cybersecurity Maturity Model Certification (CMMC): Levels 1-3 Manual
Detailed Security Control Implementation Guidance

Mark A. Russo, CISSP-ISSAP
Former Chief Information Security Officer, Department of Education

Copyright 2021, Cybersentinel, LLC, All Rights Reserved
Washington, DC ∞ Tucson, AZ

DEDICATION

This book is dedicated to my continually supportive instructors and professors at the National Defense University, Washington, DC, and their daily efforts to train and teach the next generation of cyber-warriors of this great Nation.

Copyright 2021, Cybersentinel, LLC, All Rights Reserved
Washington, DC ∞ Tucson, AZ

Cybersecurity Maturity Model Certification (CMMC): Levels 1-3 Manual
by Mark A. Russo

Copyright © 2021 Cybersentinel, LLC. All rights reserved.

Printed in the United States of America.

2021: Jan – C version

Revision History for the First Edition

Fourth version update: March 5, 2021

The Cybersentinel AI Logo is a registered trademark of Cybersentinel LLC **Cybersecurity Maturity Model Certification (CMMC): Levels 1-3 Manual.** *While the publisher and the authors have used good faith efforts to ensure that the information and instructions in this work are accurate, the publisher and the authors disclaim all responsibility for errors or omissions, including without limitation responsibility for damages resulting from the use of or reliance on this work. The use of the information and instructions contained in this work is at your own risk. Suppose any code samples or other technology this work has or describes is subject to open source licenses or others' intellectual property rights. In that case, it is your responsibility to ensure that your use thereof complies with such licenses or rights.*

FAQs

In March 2021, there were several issues answered by the DOD specific to CMMC implementation:

- **CMMC is not Retroactive.** There will be no penalties for non-compliance with existing contracts. However, future punitive actions by the government will be invoked via contract for non-conformance processes.
- **The Roll-out of CMMC is "still very fluid."** The dates and size of implementation will continue to be delayed. The DOD has not fully scoped the Level of Effort of the cost to create a non-profit company to manage and accredit the thousands of contractors that will be potentially barred from future DOD contract actions. However, companies should continue to anticipate the security control requirements, especially under the NIST 800-171 framework.
- **Mandatory CMMC certification will be required when finalized.** Contractors are still expected to be driving toward the NIST 800-171 standards. They will need to be certified by the final contract award date.
- **Acquisition Policies and Regulation Changes.** The DOC CISO has been actively engaged in several significant changes to DODI 5000-series specific to CMMC implementation. Expect them to require building security control measures to include reportable milestones and benchmarks to CMMC compliance. Additionally, DFARS changes are pending that will further mandate CMMC to have flow-down requirements to subcontractors.

Other facts:

- *There will be no foreign standards authorized under CMMC.* Under current federal law systems attaching to federal networks must comply with NIST 800-53. Those systems not directly attaching or handling federal information must comply with either NIST 800-171 or the National (NIST-based) Cybersecurity Framework. Why are you add foreign cybersecurity standards? These US standards were established because the Defense Industrial Base (DIB) continues to struggle with these frameworks. **It's the law, DOD!**

What is the major flaw of the CMMC?

The flaw is that it only secures the company's infrastructure and solves the root problem—secure system development. It should not be considered a "golden ticket" for systems developed for or on behalf of the DOD. For those systems connecting to the DOD Information Networks (DODIN), they are required to meet the regulations as described in the Federal Acquisition Regulation (FAR) and the Defense Federal Acquisition Regulation Supplement (DFARS). In this case, the system must meet NIST 800-37 and 800-53 standards. For systems not connecting to the DODIN, the systems must complete the 110 controls of NIST 800-171. CMMC will only make a portion of the supply chain secure—the Defense Industrial Base (DIB); however, it must be continuously monitored, or this will be nothing more than an old-school DOD security paperwork drill. True cybersecurity comes from *Continuous Monitoring* of the IT environment internally and externally. CMMC will not solve the entire challenge of effective cybersecurity defensive measures.

 Beware the golden-ticket-syndrome.

Check Out the
<u>Most-Extensive</u> Cybersecurity Blog Site

This is the primary resource of everything, "Cyber."
"The good, the bad, and the ugly of cybersecurity all in one place."

Join us at https://cybersentinel.tech

This free resource is available to everyone interested in the fate and future of cybersecurity in the 21st Century

Copyright 2021, Cybersentinel, LLC, All Rights Reserved
Washington, DC ∞ Tucson, AZ

2021-Version: Cybersecurity Maturity Model Certification (CMMC): Levels 1-3 Manual

Table of Contents

FAQs 5
    DOD's Cybersecurity Maturity Model Certification and NIST 800-171 17
        Who's Watching the Watchers? 18
        Expected Real CMMC Timelines 20
    Maturity is a Matter of Control Implementation 23
    NIST 800-171 Evolution 25
        Pursuing an expansion of cybersecurity standards 27
    Proof of a company's cybersecurity posture 28
        More About Artifacts and POAMs 30
    A Cybersecurity State of Mind 33
        Tailoring-out Security Controls 34
    LEVEL 1: BASIC CYBER HYGIENE CMMC Certification Controls 37
        Level 1 Control sub-set A from 48 CFR 52.204-21 38
            Why are there 15 CMMC Control duplications? 38
            The 15 CFR *Safeguarding Requirements* 40
        Level 1 Control sub-set B from NIST 800-171 42
            AC.1.001 42
            What do you need to know about Access Control? 43
            AC.1.002 44
            AC.1.003 44
            AC.1.004 46
            IA.1.076 47
            IA.1.077 47

MP.1.118 48
Supply Chain Risk Management (SCRM) in the Global IT Community 48
PE.1.131 52
PE.1.132 53
PE.1.133 53
PE.1.134 53
SC.1.175 54
SC.1.176 55
SI.1.210 55
SI.1.211 57
SI.1.212 60
SI.1.213 60
LEVEL 2: INTERMEDIATE CYBER HYGIENE CMMC Certification Controls 61
AC.2.005 62
AC.2.006 63
AC.2.007 64
3.1.5 Employ the principle of least privilege, including for specific security functions and privileged accounts. 64
AC.2.008 64
AC.2.009 65
AC.2.010 65
AC.2.011 67
AC.2.013 67
AC.2.015 68
AC.2.016 68
AU.2.041 72
Synopsis of the Audit and Accountability Control Family 72
AU.2.042 74
AU.2.043 75
AU.2.044 75
AT.2.056 76
Synopsis of Cybersecurity Awareness & Training 76
AT.2.057 78

CM.2.061 78
A Synopsis of the True Foundation of Cybersecurity 79
CM.2.062 80
CM.2.063 80
CM.2.064 81
CM.2.065 82
CM.2.066 82
IA.2.078 83
IA.2.079 85
IA.2.080 85
IA.2.081 86
IA.2.082 86
IR.2.092 87
What do you do when you are attacked? 89
IR.2.093 93
IR.2.094 94
IR.2.096 94
IR.2.097 95
MA.2.111 95
MA.2.112 96
MA.2.113 97
MA.2.114 97
MP.2.119 98
MP.2.120 98
MP.2.121 99
PS.2.127 99
PS.2.128 100
PE.2.135 100
RE.2.137 100
RE.2.138 101
RM.2.141 101
Changes to the Infrastructure 103
RM.2.142 105

- RM.2.143 105
- CA.2.157 106
- CA.2.158 106
- CA.2.159 107
- SC.2.178 107
- SC.2.179 108
- SI.2.214 109
- SI.2.216 109
- SI.2.217 110

LEVEL 3: GOOD CYBER HYGIENE CMMC Certification Controls 111

- AC.3.017 112
- *3.1.4 Separate the duties of individuals to reduce the risk of malevolent activity without collusion.* 112
- AC.3.018 112
- AC.3.019 114
- AC.3.012 114
- *3.1.17 Protect wireless access using authentication and encryption.* 114
- AC.3.020 115
- AC.3.014 115
- AC.3.021 116
- *AC.3.022* 117
- AM.3.036 117
- What is the Value of a Data Inventory? 117
- *It's time we add the Data Inventory* 118
- AU.3.045 119
- AU.3.046 119
- AU.3.048 120
- AU.3.048 120
- AU.3.049 120
- AU.3.050 120
- AU.3.051 121
- AU.3.052 122
- AT.3.058 122

CM.3.067	124
CM.3.068	124
The 5 Most Attacked Ports Survey	126
CM.3.069	128
IA.3.083	128
IA.3.084	128
IA.3.085	129
IA.3.086	129
IA.3.098	130
IA.3.099	130
MA.3.115	131
MA.3.116	131
MP.3.122	131
MP.3.123	132
MP.3.124	133
MP.3.125	133
PE.3.136	134
RE.3.139	134
RM.3.144	135
RM.3.144	135
Risk Assessment (RA) Component Template	136
RM.3.146	140
RM.3.147	140
CA.3.161	142
CA.3.162	142
SA.3.169	143
Structured Threat Information eXpression (STIX) providing External Data to Industry for Information Sharing	143
SC.3.177	144
SC.3.180	145
SC.3.181	147
SC.3.182	148
SC.3.183	148

SC.3.184 148

SC.3.185 149

SC.3.186 149

SC.3.187 150

External Certification Authority Program (ECA) 152

SC.3.188 153

SC.3.189 153

SC.3.190 154

SC.3.191 154

SC.3.192 155

SC.3.193 155

SI.3.218 156

SI.3.219 157

SI.3.220 158

CUI Classification, Marking & Storage Guide 161

Proper Marking of CUI 162

CUI Banner Markings (Reference 32 CFR 2002.20(b)) 163

CUI Banner Control Markings (Reference 32 CFR 2002.20(b)(1)) 166

CUI Categories and Subcategories (Reference 32 CFR 2002.12) 166

Banner Markings for Category and Subcategory Markings (Reference 32 CFR 2002.20(b)(2)) 168

Banner Markings with Multiple of Subcategory Markings (Reference 32 CFR 2002.20) 170

Banner Markings (Limited Dissemination Controls)(Reference 32 CFR 2002.20(b)(3) 171

Designation Indicator (Reference 32 CFR 2002.20(a)(3)(d)) 172

Portion Markings (Reference 32 CFR 2002.20(f)) 173

Portion Markings with Category Only (Reference 32 CFR 2002.20(f)) 176

Portion Markings with Category and Dissemination Caveats (Reference 32 CFR 2002.20(f)) 177

Marking of Multiple Pages (Reference 32 CFR 2002.20(c)) 180

Required Indicators as directed by Authorities (Reference 32 CFR 2002.20 (b)(2)(iii)) 181

Supplemental Administrative Markings (Reference 32 CFR 2002.20(l)) 182

- Common Mistakes for Supplemental Administrative Markings 183
- Electronic Media Storage and Marking Procedures (Reference 32 CFR 2002.20) . 184
- Marking Forms (Reference 32 CFR 2002.20) 185
- CUI Coversheets (Reference 32 CFR 2002.32) 186
- Marking Transmittal Documents (Reference 32 CFR 2002.20) 187
- Alternate Marking Methods (Reference 32 CFR 2002.20) 188
- Room or Area Markings (Reference 32 CFR 2002.20) 189
- Container Markings (Reference 32 CFR 2002.20) 190
- Shipping and Mailing (Reference 32 CFR 2002.20) 190
- Re-marking Legacy Information (Reference 32 CFR 2002.36) 191
- CUI Markings in a Classified Environment 194
  - Marking Commingled Information (Reference 32 CFR 2002.20(g)) 194
  - Commingling Portion Markings (Reference 32 CFR 2002.20(g)) 201

Appendices 203
- APPENDIX A -- RELEVANT REFERENCES 204
- APPENDIX B -- TERMS & GLOSSARY 205
- APPENDIX C – CONTINUOUS MONITORING 211
- APPENDIX D – MANAGING THE LIFECYCLE OF A POAM 226
- ABOUT THE AUTHOR 231

DOD's Cybersecurity Maturity Model Certification and NIST 800-171

> *Cybersecurity is a leadership, not a technical challenge*

In 2019, the Department of Defense (DOD) announced the *Cybersecurity Maturity Model Certification* (CMMC). The CMMC is a framework *not unlike the* National Institute of Standards and Technology (NIST) 800-171. Unfortunately, it mostly duplicates it. CMMC is nothing more than an evolution of NIST 800-171, with elements from NIST 800-53 and ISO 27001, and several other cybersecurity frameworks, to provide a better cybersecurity posture for companies and agencies conducting business with the US government. This is a positive evolution that includes and requires **third-party auditing** by cybersecurity professionals recognized by the DOD.

In addition to assessing a company's implementation of these wide-ranging cybersecurity controls, the CMMC will also evaluate its maturity/institutionalization of cybersecurity practices and processes. The **principles of cybersecurity governance** will apply security controls and their associated methodologies. These will be the rules and standards established by the DOD as the Tier 1 governing body per NIST 800-37, *Guide for Applying the Risk Management Framework (RMF) to Federal Information Systems: A Security Life Cycle Approach*, the foundational document for RMF.

 Companies will be certified at the appropriate CMMC level based upon the sensitivity of the system and its data.

> The level will be stated within formal contract requirements.
>
> CMMC also affects sub-contractors that will also be required to meet CMMC standards.

Who's Watching the Watchers?

The DOD will require third-party assessment of a company's Information Technology (IT) systems and data protection measures using most NIST controls as found in NIST 800-53 revision 4 (with revision 5 pending). Of concern, at the time of this publication, DOD is wrestling with identifying a non-profit, 503 (c) organization to lead the effort. Based on recent information, the University of Virginia's Darden school will be leading a large part of the effort to institutionalize CMMC for the DOD.

This manual predominantly follows the NIST 800-171 control implementation; however, several controls were derived from outside NIST 800-171 or NIST 800-53. This book uses a **best practice** approach to address and implement controls from the other frameworks to include ISO 27001 and others, as discussed later.

NIST 800-171 was formerly allowed for self-assessment by contractors. That has proven to be a tragedy for the DOD in its 2017 efforts under Defense Federal Acquisition Regulation Supplement (DFARS) 252.204-7012. Specifically, the CMMC does not allow this critical **weakness** of the original NIST 800-171 implementation. It recognizes that the technical capabilities of the defense contracting community have been less than complete. When it comes to an understanding of the RMF, CMMC results from historically poor cybersecurity contracting management and oversight that has plagued the DOD and the entirety of the federal government for years.

The CMMC framework arose in response to the many extreme data breaches of DOD information and weapon systems, including the F-35 Joint Strike Fighter program, where Chinese cybersecurity operations against the US have been highly successful. Further, the government's cybersecurity oversight problems included severe shortfalls in F-35 sub-systems to add its Autonomic Logistics Information System (ALIS) 3.0 in 2018. At the time, the F-35 program office has only issued a one-year *vice three-year specific* Authorization to Operate (ATO) the then existing software. The F-35 Assessment and Authorization Working Group

recommended a "high-risk ATO" to the program executive officer. The one-year ATO included 11 tasks that the program office and prime contractor must meet to maintain its cybersecurity posture. (See the full article, *F-35 JPO issues one-year ALIS 3.0 operating authority, with 11 provisions* by Ms. Courtney Albon, April 13, 2018.
https://insidedefense.com/daily-news/f-35-jpo-issues-one-year-alis-30-operating-authority-11-provisions.)

The DOD's prior reliance on the security controls in NIST 800-171 did not require third-party assessment and was presumed enough to thwart the increasing and evolving threat. However, that has been proven as a poor decision by the DOD. Contractors **will** now be required to be certified by a third-party auditor. There has been little guidance to-date of what certification a CMMC audit organization must have—**who will audit the auditors?**

Furthermore, the Defense Contract Management Agency (DCMA) and the Defense Counterintelligence and Security Agency (DCSA) will have purview over the CMMC. However, these agencies lack the current technical capabilities nor experience to execute the CMMC framework. The DCMA has stated in the past it does not have the ability, expertise, or resources to meet former NIST 800-171 mandates, and now with CMMC, the expectation is no different. However, DCMA has begun to engage with the effort and the hope they can apply the proper enforcement actions against companies that do not faithfully attempt to secure DOD-originated data.

🚫 ***The CMMC is a result of historically poor cybersecurity contracting management and oversight by the DOD that has plagued its efforts for adequate security measures for decades.***

A company or business will need to coordinate with the identified accredited and independent third-party commercial certification organization as designated by the DOD. According to Ms. Katie Arrington, DOD lead for CMMC, the target is to locate and hire a "nonprofit company" to execute auditing duties in 2020. The expectations remain low that the DOD will select, train, and certify assessors until late 2021. Furthermore, the DOD, via a contract, will choose the certification level as either high (for sensitive DOD systems), likely levels 4 through 5, to low (basic systems), likely levels 1-3.

Expected Real CMMC Timelines

Companies will be certified by late 2020 at the appropriate CMMC level based upon the system's sensitivity and data. However, as typical for the DOD in cybersecurity policy development, **expect** at least a one to a two-year delay in full implementation. The DOD has chosen to demure its responsibility and oversight, appearing to be an effort to shift risk it cannot or should not do. These positions, to avoid cybersecurity oversight, will only add to delays in CMMC implementation. [1]

Furthermore, the CMMC will include portions of various cybersecurity standards, such as NIST 800-171, ISO 270001, and ISO 27032; however, at its core, NIST 800-53 is the universally authorized standard for DOD systems. NIST 800-53/RMF will provide the basis of any rules of best security practices and a measure of the "maturity of a company's institutionalization of cybersecurity practices and processes."

The **certification cost** will become allowable as a reimbursable cost of contract negotiations under the Federal Acquisition Regulation (FAR), and more specifically, under the DFARS. While the current guidance states that the charges "will not be prohibitive," the DOD has yet to identify specified costs or tasks required to conduct auditing by third-party organizations that meet the CMMC "standard." The DOD has also not defined any cost limits or controls. This will add to low expectations for the defense

---

[1] However, the author does believe the overall CMMC objective effort is worthy of pursuing; however, the planning to-date has been poor as evident by recent selections of a Board of Directors (January 2020) where the lead stated he would make a best-faith effort to select the six remaining Board of Director members [paraphrased]. **He had no defined criteria based on a Jan 16, 2020 phone conference.**

contracting community and the associated need for tens of thousands of CMMC assessors needed for certification by 2022.

For additional and updated information, it is best to regularly check the Office of the Under Secretary of Defense for Acquisition and Sustainment website at https://www.acq.osd.mil/cmmc/index.html. The DOD plans to release Version 1.0 of CMMC by January 2020; however, expect it to be delayed as is typical for these extensive—but critical—DOD efforts. Contractors are expected to include CMMC costs in future proposals by June 2020; however, expect that to be delayed more likely into the 2021-2022 timeframes.

Office of the Under Secretary of Defense for Acquisition & Sustainment
Cybersecurity Maturity Model Certification

The Office of the Under Secretary of Defense for Acquisition and Sustainment (OUSD(A&S)) recognizes that security is foundational to acquisition and should not be traded along with cost, schedule, and performance moving forward. The Department is committed to working with the Defense Industrial Base (DIB) sector to enhance the protection of controlled unclassified information (CUI) within the supply chain.

Maturity is a Matter of Control Implementation

Maturity of security control implementation is more than a one-time evaluation of the 110 controls listed in NIST 800-171 (or any of the other major cybersecurity protection frameworks.) It relies on continuous monitoring and active oversight of changes in the IT environment. Too many "cybersecurity experts" have never administered an Authority to Operate (ATO) process and somehow have become *de jure* cybersecurity experts by proximity and not by working in "the trenches." Many "posers" and senior leaders are blinded by their lack of knowledge about risk management in general and technical control implementation. Until there is the enforcement of oversight at all levels, even the CMMC is doomed to fail.

The premise of the NIST cybersecurity process is to recognize that it is not about absolute certainty. Weak or poorly implemented security controls will not stop cyber-attacks. The foundation of risk management is about understanding the system's overall weaknesses. The company's leadership, not just the IT staff, has identified where those weaknesses exist.

Risk Management is about a defined Continuous Monitoring (ConMon) (See Appendix C) procedures and effective Risk Assessment processes. Proper processes afford the needed protection to a company's or organization's sensitive CUI/FCI. The 110 NIST 800-171 controls, for example, are not meant to be complete answers to an ever-changing risk landscape. Only through an active and continual review of the controls can DOD and companies ensure that near-certainty their networks are as secure *as possible*.

The foundation of risk management recognizes the system's overall weaknesses. It is about the company's leadership, not just the IT staff, who has identified where those weaknesses exist.

This manual provides a deep-dive understanding of the controls, how to effectively respond to the controls, and meet CMMC requirements to authorize a company to conduct business with the DOD. While DOD may be the first federal agency to mandate CMMC implementation, expect other agencies such as the Department of Homeland Security (DHS), the Department of Commerce (DOC), home of NIST, and Department of Energy (DOE), to be the next likely candidates to necessitate businesses meet CMMC-like direction and guidance.

NIST 800-171 Evolution

This manual is created to help the small and big business owners meet the newest cybersecurity contracting requirements to conduct business with the Department of Defense (DOD). The CMMC is a wide-ranging certification process with security controls most aligned with federal NIST standards. The gravest weakness of these security controls is that they tell you **what to do** but not **how to do them**. That is the purpose of this book. It provides the how-to best approach and answers the security control or at least where to fully implement the stated cybersecurity measure.

The requirement to protect information and data is limited to the financial services, insurance, and health care sectors. It is hard to identify a federal or industrial sector that escapes some responsibility to protect its electronic data. Indeed, some areas deal with more sensitive information, so it is not a surprise that the DOD recently took steps to have its contractors provide "adequate security" for "covered defense information (CDI)," which includes Controlled Unclassified Information (CUI).

Since December 31, 2017, a company that fails to have "adequate security" risks losing its contracts and ability to sell to the DoD. The CMMC is the next phase of NIST 800-171 implementation at varying levels based upon the government sponsor's sensitivity and security via contract. Consequently, government contractors have come under more significant pressure and scrutiny to explicitly comply with NIST 800-171 and associated cybersecurity policies and directives. Subcontractors face the same, if not higher, demands as part of the global supply chain connection between the direct supplier and the DOD.

> *The Council of Economic Advisers, an agency within the Executive Office of the President, estimates that malicious cyber activity cost the U.S. economy between $57 billion and $109 Billion in 2016*
> [Source: The Cost of Malicious Cyber Activity to the U.S. Economy, CEA, 2018]

The guidance, "DoD Guidance for Reviewing System Security Plans and the NIST SP 800-171 Security Requirements Not Yet Implemented," was issued by NIST. The direction is characterized as a tool to help the DoD and contractors assess their System Security Plans (SSPs) and Plans of Action (POA)/Plans of Action and Milestones (POAM) and to prioritize what steps should be undertaken to satisfy the DFARS 252.204-7012 mandate for "adequate security." (See Appendix D: Managing the Lifecycle of a POAM).

DOD guidance also addresses methods by which the security requirements that have not been met may be implemented. When applicable, the direction provides additional clarification to the company or business. Methods of implementation may include reconfiguring the IT system, the procurement of hardware and software, or developing written corporate policies and procedures. This guidance will better enable DOD, and Nonfederal Organization (NFO), specifically businesses, to prioritize and address any gaps in their cybersecurity program in the context of the CMMC standards and deploy appropriate information security controls more structured and efficient manner.

The new direction also provides government personnel and its contractors' further objective criteria to measure whether a third-party provider, to include the growing Cloud Service Provider (CSP) community, good cybersecurity program that will protect the confidentiality, integrity, and availability of its respective stores of CUI/FCI. The guidance further demonstrates which businesses have implemented a holistic cybersecurity program and those who have not to the DOD and beyond.

Pursuing an expansion of cybersecurity standards

Historical and regular intrusions into critical federal systems point to the ever agile and highly impactful effects of cyber-threats worldwide. Reports of the large volumes of personal data exfiltrated from the Office of Personnel Management (OPM) and intrusions into seemingly highly protected DOD networks highlight the need for change. "For nearly a week, some 4,000-key military and civilian personnel working for the Joint Chiefs of Staff [had] lost access to their unclassified email after what is now believed to be an intrusion into the critical Pentagon server that handles that email network..." (Starr, B., 2015, July 31. The military is still dealing with cyber-attack 'mess.' Retrieved from CNN.com: http://www.cnn.com/2015/07/31/politics/defense-department-computer-intrusion-email-server/)

The need to implement and enhance the RMF based on NIST's cybersecurity-focused 800-series continues to be highly debated. The challenge has been about expanding the NIST RMF "framework" beyond the federal government's multiple IT security boundaries. What if the federal government mandated its applicability to the private sector? Can the expansion of the CMMC provide a strategic means to protect the Nation's sensitive data?

This also includes enhancing laws and regulations to increase corporate and business cybersecurity protections; this comprises current legislation such as the Federal Information Security Management Act (FISMA) of 2002 and was updated by Congress in 2014. These laws, regulations, and processes will hopefully improve and protect the critical infrastructures and sensitive data stored within the US's physical boundaries and vital corporations. Presumably, such an evolution will better protect the US's vital and sensitive data from internal and foreign state actors desiring to harm the US.

Congress wrote FISMA to reduce the effectiveness of cyber-attacks against the federal government and its vast IT infrastructure. FISMA and other cybersecurity laws provide a needed method to enhance oversight of information security applications, systems, and networks. FISMA further explicitly sought to "...provide a comprehensive framework for ensuring the effectiveness of information security controls over information resources that support Federal operations and assets" (US Government, 2002). Federal Information Security Management Act of 2002 (44 U.S.C. §§ 3541-3549). It is retrieved from NIST: http://csrc.nist.gov/drivers/documents/FISMA-final.pdf.

In 2014, DOD internally adopted the NIST RMF 800-series as the standard. The overall effort has become the current DOD direction and guidance to protect its own critical IT infrastructure more effectively and expand beyond its boundaries to protect *its* data transmitted into the private sector.

NIST 800-171 revision 1 was the first attempt for DOD that applies to vendors and contractors to ensure CUI/FCI is appropriately protected from threats; the introduction of the CMMC is the codification of 800-171 formally. It is further mandated that information about a company's business specific to the DOD is protected from compromise or exploit a modification, loss, or destruction. DOD is attempting to ensure an essential effort is executed to protect the company's own internal CUI//FCI as well as co-mingled DOD information that is created as part of the company's regular business operations.

Proof of a company's cybersecurity posture

The basis of CMMC is that contractors provide adequate security on all covered contractor Information Systems (IS). Typically, the minimum requirement to demonstrate control implementation is through documentation. Another term that is used throughout this book is an artifact. An artifact is any representation to an independent third-party assessor that shows compliance with specific security control. It is a significant part of the proof that a business owner would provide DOD.

The common term for collecting all applications and supporting artifacts is the Body of Evidence (BOE). The necessary items required for the BOE includes three major elements:

1. **Company Policy or Procedure.** For this book, these terms are used interchangeably. Substantially any direction provided to internal employees and subcontractors that are enforceable under United States (US) labor laws and Human Resource (HR) direction. It is recommended that such a policy or procedure artifact be a unique collection of how the company addresses each of the controls through the CMMC; this book will *only* focus on Levels 1-3 as changes are expected to be released for the higher levels of security maturity in late 2020.

> *All policy or procedure requirements are best captured in a single business policy or procedure guide. This should address the controls aligned with the security control families.*

---

2. **System Security Plan (SSP).** This is a standard cybersecurity document. It describes the company's overall IT infrastructure to include hardware and software lists. Where appropriate, suggestions of additional artifacts included in this document and duplicated into a DOD standard SSP format will be recommended. It is best to request standard formats through the supporting contract office to avoid delays in contract issuance.

   A *free* 36-minute introduction to the SSP is currently available on Udemy.com at https://www.udemy.com/system-security-plan-ssp-for-nist-800-171-compliance/.

3. **Plans of Action and Milestones (POAM).** These describe any control that the company cannot fix or fully demonstrate its full compliance with the control. It provides an opportunity for a company to delay addressing a difficult to implement a technical solution or prohibitive cost.

   POAMs should always have an expected completion date and defined interim milestones (typically monthly) that describe the actions leading to a full resolution or implementation of the control. *POAMs usually should not be for more than a year; however, a critical hint, a company can request an extension multiple times if unable to fully meet the control.*

When working with the government, being simple, aligned (with the stated security controls) and consistent will help through a very young and undefined process.

More About Artifacts and POAMs

    Other artifacts that are strongly suggested including the collection of **screen captures.** All current Operating Systems (OS) include a "print screen" function where the text or image is captured, placed in temporary computer memory, and can be easily inserted into other locations or hard copy printed. IT personnel should use this function to show, for example, policy settings and system logging (audit) data. When in doubt, always have some form of graphical representation to show the assessor.

    The POAM will be used where the business cannot meet or address the control either for technical reasons, "we do not have a Data at Rest

(DAR) encryption program," or cost, "we plan to purchase the DAR solution No Later Than April 1, 2019." POAMs should include milestones; milestones should describe what will be accomplished over time to prepare for the full implementation of the control in the future. What will the business do in the interim to address the control? This could include, for example, other mitigation responses of using improved physical security controls, such as a 24-7 guard force, the addition of a steel-door to prevent entry to the main computer servers, or improved and enforceable policies that have explicit repercussions upon personnel.

POAMs will always have a defined end date. Typically, it is either within 90 days, six months, or a year in length. For DOD, one year should be the maximum date; however, as part of this fledgling process, the business can request an extension to the POAM past the "planned" end date. RMF affords such flexibilities; do not be afraid to exercise them as appropriate. (See the sample below).

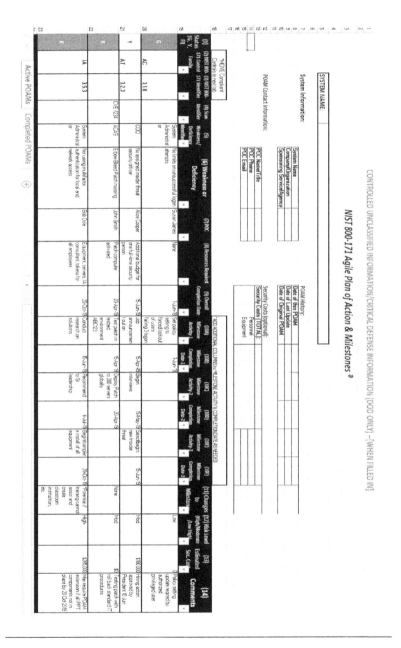

Sample POAM Template

A Cybersecurity State of Mind

This book also suggests a mental model and approach to understanding what the *security controls are* (and are not). The first paragraph following the designated control will describe a MINIMUM ANSWER. This is needed to prepare a base answer for a minimal and acceptable response to cybersecurity measures sought under the CMMC. Solutions are predominantly policy-based documents that describe to the government how the business will ensure this control will be met; if just trying to get through the process expeditiously, this paragraph will be enough to secure approval. An example of control may be found below.

CMMC-C001/P1001 (Duplicates CFR-1)

NIST 800-171-3.1.1[2] *Limit information system access to authorized users, processes acting on behalf of authorized users, or devices (including other information systems).*

MINIMUM ANSWER: Address this control in the business policy/procedural document. (See example procedure below).

It should identify the types of users and what level of access they are authorized. Typically, some general users have regular daily access to the corporate system data and **elevated/privileged users**.

Elevated/privileged users are usually limited to, for example, System Administrators (SA), Database Administrators (DBA), and other designated Help Desk IT support staff personnel who manage the back-office care of the system; these users usually have **root access**. Root access provides what is more typically described as **super-user** access. These individuals should be highly and regularly screened....

MORE COMPLETE ANSWER: This should include screen captures that show a sample of employees and their types and kinds of access rights. This could consist of their read, write, edit, delete, etc., **rights** typically controlled by an assigned SA.

---

[2] This XX.XX.XX control will map directly to NIST 800-171A.

> *We have provided an example of a suggested procedure for this control….*

If there is a greater desire to understand the process further and demonstrate a more robust solution, the paragraph, MORE COMPLETE ANSWER, is designed to provide more depth. It is intended to more completely describe to the system owner how to understand DOD's implementation of the CMMC better.

Tailoring-out Security Controls

The 2016 version update to NIST 800-171, revision 1, provided an *inadequate* direction on **control tailoring**. It states in Appendix E that there are three primary criteria for the removal of security control (or control enhancement):

- **The control is uniquely federal (i.e., primarily the federal government's responsibility):** DOD directly provides the company's control. While possible, expect this not typically to occur.
- **The control is not directly related to protecting the confidentiality of CUI/FCI:** This will also not apply since all these controls were initially chosen to safeguard all CUI/FCI confidentiality. That is why this book exists to explain better how to address these controls, which are, for the most part, all required.
- **The control is expected to be routinely satisfied by Nonfederal Organizations (NFO) without specification:** In other words, the control is expected to be met by the NFO, i.e., the company (you and your IT team.)

Tailoring is wholly allowed and recommended where appropriate. Within the NIST/CMMC cybersecurity frameworks, the concept of **tailoring-out** of a control is desirable, where technically or operationally, it cannot be reasonably applied. This will require technical certainty that the control is Non-Applicable (N/A). Under this opportunity, if the company's IT architecture does not contain within its **security boundary,** the technology where such a control would be required to be applied when the control is identified as N/A.

Tailoring-out can be your friend.

For example, where the business has no Wi-Fi network in its security boundary, it can advise the government that any controls addressing its Wi-Fi security would be a N/A control. The business cannot nor have reason to implement this control because it currently does not allow Wi-Fi networks or any presence of such equipment such as Wi-Fi routers, antennas, etc. The control would be marked as **compliant** and annotated as N/A at the time of the self-assessment. It would still be required to identify that Wi-fi is not currently authorized in the company's cybersecurity procedure guide or policy.

Good Processes Provide Good Test Artifact Outputs— If there are none, then the process has NO value.

The author has added a "scissor" ✂ icon for potential controls that may likely be tailored out. They will not be required if they are technically not present or needed to be implemented based on IT architecture. State the control as Non-Applicable (NA) in any the System Security Plan (SSP) and POAM document as directed.

This icon denotes suggested language that can be included in either the company's SSP, cybersecurity policy, or both. This will drive the Plan of Action and Milestones (POAM).

LEVEL 1: BASIC CYBER HYGIENE

CMMC Certification Controls
32 Security Controls (→ 17 actual)

Level 1 Control sub-set A from 48 CFR 52.204-21

When does 32 = 17?

Why are there 15 CMMC Control duplications?

Security controls MUST be either:
- Technically implemented
- Addressed in a cybersecurity policy document, or
- A Plan of Action and Milestone (POAM) must be created.

This first subset of controls addresses the basic safeguarding of Covered Contractor Information Systems to include Controlled Unclassified Information (CUI), Controlled Defense Information (CDI)[3], and Federal Contract Information (FCI). The CMMC requires 15 security controls from 48 CFR 52.204-21--which duplicate the 17 NIST 800-171 existing controls under Level I CMMC certification. **There are ONLY 17 security controls in CMMC Level I.**

Why the confusion? The personnel working on this policy have little understanding or quality control measures to oversee accurate cybersecurity protection measures. While the author has great respect for the two institutions assisting in the formulation of the CMMC, it is apparent that there are severe gaps in the current expertise. There is a lack of cybersecurity professionals who genuinely understand what NIST 800 and CMMC cybersecurity protections controls mean and how they provide cybersecurity protection measures. There is a continued failure, and the CMMC is just one new attempt to fix the broken state of DOD and federal cybersecurity. For this reason, the author in no way is critical of the strategic *but* the tactical efforts executed by the DOD to-date.

---

[3] CDI is a former term under consideration within the DOD to replace For Official Use Only (FOUO). With the advent of CMMC, the term CUI is used for what was formerly marked as FOUO. FOUO and CUI are non-national defense security information.

Additionally, the Prime Contractor is required to include the substance of this clause in subcontracts, i.e., "flow-down requirements," under a DOD contract. This includes subcontracts for the acquisition of commercial items other than commercially available off-the-shelf items. The subcontractor may have Federal contract information residing in or transiting through its Information System (IS).

Definitions:

"*Covered contractor information system" means an information system owned or operated by a contractor that processes, stores, or transmits Federal contract information.*

"*Federal Contract Information (FCI)" means information, not intended for public release, that is provided by or generated for the Government under a contract to develop or deliver a product or service to the Government, but not including information provided by the Government to the public (such as on public Web sites) or simple transactional information, such as necessary to process payments.*

"*Information" means any communication or representation of knowledge such as facts, data, or opinions, in any medium or form, including textual, numerical, graphic, cartographic, narrative, or audiovisual.*

"*Information system" means a discrete set of information resources organized for collecting, processing, maintenance, use, sharing, dissemination, or disposition of information.*

"*Safeguarding" means measures or controls that are prescribed to protect information systems.*

The reader may proceed to the next section since the 15 controls below are duplicates under CMMC certification Level I.

The 15 CFR *Safeguarding Requirements*

(All of the CFR controls map directly to NIST 800-171 controls as found in the next section; they are only provided here for context).

The Contractor shall apply the following basic safeguarding requirements and procedures to protect covered contractor information systems. They are provided only as a reference for this section. **They are duplicated and mapped directly to existing NIST 800-171 controls in the next section and may be skipped.**

- **CFR-1:** Limit information system access to authorized users, processes acting on behalf of authorized users, or devices (including other information systems). **(NIST 800-171 – AC 3.1.1)**
- **CFR-2:** Limit information system access to the types of transactions and functions that authorized users can execute. **(AC 3.1.2)**
- **CFR-3:** Verify and control/limit connections to and use of external information systems. **(AC 3.1.20)**
- **CFR-4:** Control information posted or processed on publicly accessible information systems. **(AC 3.1.22)**
- **CFR-5:** Identify information system users, processes acting on behalf of users, or devices. **(IA 3.5.1)**
- **CFR-6:** Authenticate (or verify) the identities of those users, processes, or devices as a prerequisite to allowing access to organizational information systems. **(IA 3.5.2)**
- **CFR-7:** Sanitize or destroy information system media containing Federal Contract Information before disposal or release for reuse. **(MP 3.8.3)**
- **CFR-8:** Limit physical access to organizational information systems, equipment, and the respective operating environments to authorized individuals. **(PP- 3.10.1)**
- **CFR-9:** Escort visitors and monitor visitor activity; maintain audit logs of physical access; and control and manage physical access devices. **(PP- 3.10.3, 3.10.4, 3.10.5)**
- **CFR-10:** Monitor, control, and protect organizational communications (*i.e.,* information transmitted or received by organizational information systems) at the external boundaries and key internal boundaries of the information systems. **(SC 3.13.1)**

- **CFR-11:** Implement subnetworks for publicly accessible system components that are physically or logically separated from internal networks. **(SC 3.13.5)**

- **CFR-12:** Identify, report, and correct information and information system flaws in a timely manner. **(SI 3.14.1)**

- **CFR-13:** Provide protection from malicious code at appropriate locations within organizational information systems. **(SI 3.14.2)**

- **CFR-14:** Update malicious code protection mechanisms when new releases are available. **(SI 3.14.4)**

- **CFR-15:** Perform periodic scans of the information system and real-time scans of files from external sources as files are downloaded, opened, or executed. **(SI 3.14.5)**

Level 1 Control sub-set B from NIST 800-171

These are the 17 security controls drawn from CMMC version 1.0 FINAL, January 31, 2020.

AC.1.001

<u>NIST 800-171-3.1.1</u>[4] *Limit information system access to authorized users, processes acting on behalf of authorized users, or devices (including other information systems).*

MINIMUM ANSWER: Address this control in the business policy/procedural document. (See example procedure below).

It should identify the types of users and what level of access they are authorized. Typically, some general users have regular daily access to the corporate system data and **elevated/privileged users**.

Elevated/privileged users are usually limited to, for example, System Administrators (SA), Database Administrators (DBA), and other designated Help Desk IT support staff personnel who manage the back-office care of the system; these users usually have **root access**. Root access provides what is more typically described as **super-user** access. These individuals should be highly and regularly screened. These individuals need to be periodically assessed or audited by senior corporate designated personnel.

MORE COMPLETE ANSWER: This should include screen captures that show a sample of employees and their types and kinds of access rights. This could consist of their read, write, edit, delete, etc., **rights** typically controlled by an assigned SA.

We have provided an example of a suggested procedure for this control:

EXAMPLE PROCEDURE: *The company has defined two types of authorized users. There are general users, those that require regular daily access to company automated*

---

[4] This maps directly to NIST 800-171A.

> resources, and privileged users, employees with elevated privileges required to conduct proper back-office care and maintenance of corporate assets and Information Technology (IT) systems. Access to the company's [example] financial, ordering, and human resource systems will be restricted to those general users who need to access these systems based upon their duties. Immediate supervisors will validate their needs and advise the IT Help Desk to issue appropriate access credentials [login identification and password] after completing "Cybersecurity Awareness Training." User credentials will not be shared, and…."

What do you need to know about Access Control?

The initial set of controls is derived from NIST Access Control (AC) controls designed to restrict individual's access based upon rights as described in any organization's cybersecurity policy. There is two major division of rights:

1. Basic user
2. Privileged Users

The AC control family is the most technical and most vital security controls within the cybersecurity process. It is designed to focus computer support personnel, System Administrators (SA), or similar IT staff on critical data's technical security protections. This will include CUI/FCI and internal sensitive data maintained by its IT infrastructure and the company as part of doing business with the DOD. If making investments in cybersecurity infrastructure upgrades, the **AC** *controls will* **provide the highest Return on Investment (ROI).**

It is critical to confirm whether either technical solution is not already embedded in the current IT system. Often, controls are ignored, captured by policy, or a POAM is developed, even though some base capabilities to address the control are already resident in the IT system or, more particularly, within the network Operating System (OS). Check for accessory applications provided by the OS manufacturer to determine whether a no-cost solution is already resident. Ask the IT staff to confirm whether there is an existing technical solution to avoid spending additional dollars for capabilities already in place.

Where cost is prohibitive to implement a POAM, a POAM is an acceptable but temporary solution. If unable to address the control during the company's implementation efforts, formulate a Plans of Action and Milestone (POAM). (See Appendix D: Managing the Lifecycle of a POAM).

AC.1.002

3.1.2 Limit information system access to the types of transactions and functions that authorized users are permitted to execute.

MINIMUM ANSWER: Address this control in the business policy/procedural document. It should identify the types of transactions and what level is allowed for authorized users. Elevated or privileged users have access to back-office maintenance and care of the network such as account creation, database maintenance, etc.; privileged users can also have general access, but different logins and passwords should segregate their privileges for audit purposes.

MORE COMPLETE ANSWER: This could include a screen capture that shows a sample of employees and their types and kinds of rights. This would consist of their read, write, edit, delete, etc., rights typically controlled by assigned SA. The SA should provide the hardcopy printouts for inclusion into the final submission packet to the DOD contract office or their designated recipient.

AC.1.003

3.1.20 Verify and control/limit connections to and use of external systems.

MINIMUM ANSWER: This control requires that all external or third-party connections to the company's network be verified. This would typically take the form of accepting another company (or even DOD agencies') Authority to Operate (ATO). This could be as simple as a memorandum, for example, recognizing another company's CMMC approved packet from a third-party assessment organization.

This process is known as **reciprocity** of accepting an ATO allowed under RMF—more typical of DOD and other federal agencies. These are all legitimate means that are designed to ensure a company allows another company to enter through its *firewall* (system security boundary); before an external system or network is allowed unfettered access to the corporations' data, it is critical to identify the rules and restrictions for such access as part of this control.

Ensure procedures identify and limit connections to only critical data feeds needed from third-party[5] companies and consultants to conduct formal business operations.

MORE COMPLETE ANSWER: This could include a request for ongoing scans of the external system or network every 30 days; this would be considered quite extreme but dependent on data sensitivity. If sought, suggest that every six-month that the company receives copies of the anti-virus, anti-malware, and vulnerability patch scanning reports identifying current threats to the external system. This is designed to address inbound threats potentially and to enhance the company's overall security posture.

EXAMPLE PROCEDURE: "The ABC IT System is a self-contained system with secure connectivity pathways to the Internet through a commercial Delta Internet Service Provider (ISP) connection. These connections are continuously monitored using the ISP's commercial security solutions, including the firewall. The ABC IT System uses resident Windows' *Essential Security against Evolving Threat Events* (ESET) End-point Security solution. ESET capabilities include real-time anti-virus, anti-spyware, anti-spam, anti-malware detection and prevention devices."

---

[5] Do not confuse this term for third-party with the formal assessors of an organization's IT system.

AC.1.004

3.1.22 Control CUI posted or processed on publicly accessible systems.

MINIMUM ANSWER: This addresses the control of publicly accessible information, most commonly on the company's **public-facing** website. There needs to be procedural guidance and direction about who can release (usually public affairs office, etc.) and post information (usually webmaster, etc.) to the website. This should include a review of such data by personnel specially trained to recognize CUI/FCI data. This may include information or data that discusses a company's current business relationship with the DOD, the activities it conducts, and the products and services it provides to both the public and private sectors.

This should also address the regular review of publicly accessible data and the procedure to describe the process to remove unauthorized data if discovered.

MORE COMPLETE ANSWER: This could use automated scans of keywords and phrases that may alert audit personnel during their regular auditing activities. While this is a static means to alert untrained IT personnel, it could supplement that inadvertent release does not occur. Additional oversight should always be based upon the sensitivity of the information handled to include CUI/FCI but Intellectual Property (IP) or other sensitive data. That may harm the company if released to the public.

The decision process of how much encryption and added protection (such as hashing or emerging blockchain encryption technologies) should be based on the IT system's risk.

Consider the risk and the damage to the company if the data, CUI//FCI are compromised

---

IA.1.076

3.5.1 Identify information system users, processes acting on behalf of users, or devices.

MINIMUM/MORE COMPLETE ANSWER: This control should identify/reference current business cybersecurity policies or procedures. It should address that audits are used to identify system users, the processes (applications), and the devices (computers) accessed.

IA.1.077

3.5.2 Authenticate (or verify) the identities of those users, processes, or devices, as a prerequisite to allowing access to organizational information systems.

MINIMUM ANSWER: While basic logon and password information could be used, Control 3.5.3 requires Multifactor or Two-factor Authentication (2FA). DOD requires 2FA, and CMMC requires it.

Remember, if the company is not immediately prepared to execute a 2FA solution, *a POAM is required*.

MORE COMPLETE ANSWER: The better answer is the employment of some form of 2FA. It could be a **hard token** solution such as a CAC or PIV card. The other option would include virtual solutions that would use email or SMS messaging like Google ® or Amazon ® to provide 2FA; this **soft token** solution is typically easier and less expensive to deploy. It can be more easily used to meet these DOD and CMMC requirements.

MP.1.118

3.8.3 Sanitize or destroy information system media containing CUI before disposal or release for reuse.

MINIMUM ANSWER: A good policy description is a must regarding data destruction of sensitive information within DOD. Either use a commercial-grade "wiping" program or physically destroy the drive.

If the company plans to internally reuse or sell to outside repurposing companies, ensure that the wiping is a commercial grade or approved by DOD. There are companies providing disk shredding or destruction services. Provide any service agreements that should specify the type and level of data destruction to DOD assessors.

MORE COMPLETE ANSWER: For any DOD assessment, the media sanitization company should provide **destruction certificates**. Chose several selected destruction certificates to include in the DOD BOE submission. Typically, the business's logistics and supply ordering sections should manage as part of the Supply Chain Risk Management (SCRM) process.

Supply Chain Risk Management (SCRM) in the Global IT Community

SCRM is a relatively new concern within the federal government. It is part of securing IT products within the business.

Questions that should be considered include:

- Is this product produced by the US or by an Ally?
- Could counterfeit IT items be purchased from less-than-reputable entities?
- Is this IT product from an approved hardware/software product listing?

Users innately trust software developers to provide security updates for their software applications and products that would add new functionalities or fix security vulnerabilities. They would not expect updates to be infected with malicious scripts, codes, or programming. Most users have no mechanisms (or no concerns) about defending against seemingly legitimate software that is duly signed. Unfortunately, software unwittingly accessed by users and tainted by either nation-state actors or general cyber-criminals on the Internet poses an alarming risk to the global IT supply chain.

The use of varied supply chain attacks by cyber attackers to access corporate software development infrastructures has been a significant vector of concerns for the government and the private sector. These attacks typically include targeting publicly connected software build, test, update servers, and other portions of a software company's software development environment. Nation-state agents can inject malware into software updates, and releases have far-ranging impacts on the IT supply chain; the challenge continues to grow.[6]

Users become infected through official software distribution channels that are trusted. Attackers can add their malware to software vendors' development infrastructure before they are compiled[7]; hence, the malware is signed with the digital identity of a legitimate software vendor. This exploit bypasses typical "whitelisting" security measures making it difficult to identify the intrusion. This has contributed to a high degree of success by malicious cyber threat actors. Some example recent intrusions include:

> **Special Topic: DOD USB Policy**
>
> A UNIVERSAL SERIAL BUS (USB) OR **THUMB DRIVE** WHILE PROVIDING GREAT FLEXIBILITY TO MOVE DATA TO AND FROM SYSTEM DATA STORES, THEY ARE ALSO MAJOR MEANS TO INJECT MALICIOUS SOFTWARE SUCH AS VIRUSES AND RANSOMWARE INTO A COMPANY'S SECURITY BOUNDARY. DOD PROHIBITS USB USE IN DOD ENVIRONMENTS. IT'S CRITICAL TO ADDRESS THE PROPER CARE AND USE OF THESE IN A COMPANY'S IT INFRASTRUCTURE AND ASSOCIATED PROCEDURE GUIDE.

---

[6] Other less-protected portions of the supply chain include, for example, Field Programmable Gate Arrays (FPGA) and Application-Specific Integrated Circuit (ASIC) chips found on most major US weapons and satellite systems.

[7] Before they are converted as an executable (.exe) they are injected at the programming level where quality control mechanisms are often less adequate in secure development processes.

- In July 2017, Chinese cyber espionage operatives changed the software packages of a legitimate software vendor, NetSarang Computer (https://www.netsarang.com/). These changes allowed access to a broad range of industries and institutions that included retail locations, financial services, transportation, telecommunications, energy, media, and academics.

- In August 2017, hackers inserted a backdoor into updates of the computer "cleanup" program, **CCleaner**, while in its software development phases.

- In June 2017, suspected Russian actors deployed the PETYA ransomware to a wide-range of European targets by compromising a targeted Ukrainian software vendor.

Supply chain compromises have been ongoing for years. However, they have been remote and covert[8]. They may follow with follow-on intrusions of targets later and provide a means for general hacking and damage to the company targets. The use of such compromises offers likely means for support nation-state cyber espionage, including those identified from Chinese IT equipment product producers and manufacturers. These include such companies, such as Chinese-based companies include ZTE, Lenovo, and Huawei.

This trend continues to grow as more points in the supply chain can penetrate the attackers using advanced techniques. The techniques involved have become publicly discussed enough. Their proven usefulness encourages others to use these vectors of attack specific to damage and reconnaissance of governments, businesses, and agencies globally. Advanced actors will likely continue to leverage this activity to conduct cyber espionage, cybercrime, and disruption. The dangers to the supply chain are of growing concern as the threat and risk landscapes continue to increase for the foreseeable future.

See NIST 800-161, Supply Chain Risk Management Practices for Federal Information Systems and Organizations for further information. (http://nvlpubs.nist.gov/nistpubs/SpecialPublications/NIST.SP.800-161.pdf).

ALSO, SEE THE AUTHOR'S BOOK ON SCRM FOR GREATER DETAILS:

---

[8] Disclosing such information by a business may have both legal and reputation impacts; current US law under the 2015 Computer Information Security Act (CISA) does allow for "safe harbor" protections in the US.

A GUIDE FOR SUPPLY CHAIN RISK MANAGEMENT (SCRM) APPLICATION IN THE REAL WORLD. Welcome to the next iteration of SCRM. From the internationally acclaimed cybersecurity thought-leader, Mr. Russo provides two distinct NIST 800-161, "Supply Chain Risk Management Practices for Federal Information Systems and Organizations," approaches to resolving the modern-day challenge of SCRM. The solutions, while similar, provide a 21st Century resolution to a better approach in a systematic way to prevent compromises to the US and global IT supply chain. The use of varied supply chain attacks by cyber attackers to access, for example, software development infrastructures, has been a significant vector of concern for governments and the private sector. These attacks typically include targeting publicly connected software "build, test, update servers" and other portions of a software development environment. Nation-state agents can then inject malware into software updates, and subsequent releases have far-ranging impacts on the IT supply chain; the challenge continues to grow. SCRM 1.0 is a concept for establishing an effective and repeatable process applied against standard supply chain components such as hardware, firmware, software, etc. The author introduces SCRM 2.0, much like SCRM 1.0 (Product-based approach); the need is to turn to a much more precarious aspect of SCRM. We must consider the service piece of SCRM that includes the people, companies, and organizations along the supply chain that may also be compromised within the global marketing of IT equipment and capabilities. This is the next most significant issue facing the field of cybersecurity protection in the 21st Century.

PE.1.131

3.10.1 Limit physical access to organizational information systems, equipment, and the respective operating environments to authorized individuals.

MINIMUM ANSWER: Of importance for this control is limiting access to corporate data servers, backup devices, and specifically, the "computer farm." If the company maintains devices on its premises, the policy should address who has authorized access to such sensitive areas.

Suppose the corporation is using an off-site Cloud Service Provider (CSP), capture in part or full sections of any CSP service agreements such as a Cloud Service Level Agreement (CSLA). In that case, this should include any specific actions and control measures for any physical security protection.

Both types of computer architectures, on-premise, and cloud should address. For example, such areas of interest include access logs, after-hours access, camera monitoring, unauthorized access reporting criteria, types, and network defense devices such as Intrusion Detection and Prevention Systems (IDS/IPS), etc., as part of the corporate procedure.

MORE COMPLETE ANSWER: This could include active alerting to both management and security personnel that includes phone calls, email alerts, or SMS text messages to designated company security personnel. Security measures and **alert thresholds** should be driven by the sensitivity of the data stored. Management should make **risk-based** determinations of the cost and returns on effectiveness to drive the corporate policy for this control and other solutions.

EXAMPLE PROCEDURE: "All personnel will be briefed on physical access and the protection of systems, equipment, and respective operating environments by authorized personnel. All personnel will sign the most current version of the Security Protection Plan (SPP). Disciplinary action will be referred to Company leadership and action via the prime contractor's Program Manager of Record and the Company's PM."

Document, document, document

PE.1.132

3.10.3 Escort visitors and monitor visitor activity.

MINIMUM ANSWER: Have a section in the company's cybersecurity policy a discussion of visitor control. This should always include requiring all non-employees to be escorted to include janitorial staff, consultants, and supply vendors.

MORE COMPLETE ANSWER: To improve upon the policy, including sign-in sheets, retention and destruction requirements, and minimum background and security checks for visitors to include third-party vendors and consultants.

PE.1.133

3.10.4 Maintain audit logs of physical access.

MINIMUM/MORE COMPLETE ANSWER: Refer to Control 3.10.3 for suggested audit log items. This should also address personnel during operating and after-hour entry into the company and its IT facilities. This includes logs specific to outside third-party vendors and subcontractors; any such procedures should apply to those individuals who are not direct employees.

PE.1.134

3.10.5 Control and manage physical access devices.

MINIMUM ANSWER: This control requires that physical access devices such as security badges, combinations, and physical keys are managed through both procedures and logs (physical or automated). The company needs to demonstrate to the government its positive security measures to protect its CUI/FCI data. While this control may appear more manageable than its technical policy control settings for its IT systems, it is no less critical.

MORE COMPLETE ANSWER: If not already in place, identify and separate the physical security functions (e.g., facility security officer, etc.) from the technical security functions managed by corporate IT personnel with requisite skills and experiences. Companies should avoid duty-creep on their cybersecurity personnel and define roles and responsibilities between its classic security functions (e.g., physical, personnel security, etc.). Its roles and responsibilities will reduce their effectiveness in both security areas.

Cybersecurity workforce duty-creep is a real-world occurrence; Companies are unwittingly shifting overall "security" functions from classic security personnel to cybersecurity professionals creating overall security gaps for a company or agency

SC.1.175

3.13.1 Monitor, control, and protect organizational communications (i.e., information transmitted or received by organizational information systems) at the external boundaries and key internal boundaries of the information systems.

MINIMUM ANSWER: This control can be answered in the corporate procedure and include, for example, active auditing that checks for unauthorized access, individuals (external) who have had numerous failed logins, and traffic entering the network from "blacklisted" addresses, etc. The company should refer to its specific audit procedures

MORE COMPLETE ANSWER: This control could be better met as formerly discussed using "smart" firewalls and advanced Security Incident Event Managers (SIEM) solutions. While costlier and requiring more technical experience, corporate leadership should consider it. While not necessarily cost-effective for the current state of the company, these solutions should be regarded as part of any future architectural change effort. Any planning efforts should consider current and future technology purchases meant to enhance the company's cybersecurity posture. See Appendix C for a broader description of SIEM technologies and how they may become part of the IT infrastructure.

SC.1.176

3.13.5 Implement subnetworks for publicly accessible system components that are physically or logically separated from internal networks.

MINIMUM/MORE COMPLETE ANSWER: The most straightforward answer is that subnetworks reduce an intruder's ability to exploit corporate network addresses effectively. Have IT personnel establish subnetworks specifically for the email and webservers that are in the *external* Demilitarized Zone (DMZ) of the corporation's security boundary; see Control 3.14.2 for the location of a DMZ relative to the company's network. Some companies maintain external database servers; ensure they, too, have established subnetwork addresses.

SI.1.210

3.14.1 Identify, report, and correct information and information system flaws promptly.

MINIMUM ANSWER: This control addresses what are considered security-relevant flaws. These would include, for example, software patches, hotfixes, anti-virus, and anti-malware signatures.

Typically, network Operating Systems can check with manufacturers via the Internet for updates, e.g., "security patches" in near-real-time. It is essential to allow patches from the authorized manufacturers and sources to be updated as soon as possible. They usually are designed to fix bugs and minor through significant security vulnerabilities. The sooner the system is updated, the better. Ensure a process, such as checks by IT personnel, at least twice a day. Many systems will allow for automated "pushes" to the network. Ensure that documented processes account for IT personnel review to "audit" known pushes by only authorized sources.

Major DOD Security Events/Zero-Day Attacks: There are times that the federal government becomes aware of **zero-day attacks**. These are attacks where there is no current security patch and sometimes require other actions by DOD-supported organizations and corporations; be mindful of these events from DOD and Department of Homeland Security (DHS) alerts. These will require near-immediate action. Furthermore, DOD may direct everyone, including CMMC businesses, to report their status to the Contract Officer by an established deadline.

MORE COMPLETE ANSWER: Ensure that designated IT personnel are aware of and monitor the active vulnerabilities sites from both DOD and the DHS. A dynamic process to verify the current state of threats against DOD is an excellent means to establish a company's due diligence in this area. Check with your Contract Officer (KO/CO) for this information early during the question submission phase of contracting.

DHS's United States Computer Emergency Readiness Team (US-CERT) has the latest information on vulnerabilities to include zero-day updates. It is also recommended that designated IT personnel sign up for the Rich Site Summary (RSS) data feeds by selecting the left's symbol. The address for the site is: https://www.us-cert.gov/ncas/current-activity

SI.1.211

3.14.2 Provide protection from malicious code at appropriate locations within organizational information systems.

MINIMUM ANSWER: Protecting the network from malicious code is typically through both active anti-virus and malware protection applications or services. Ensure if additional protections provided by the businesses' commercial ISP are included in any artifact submission.

MORE COMPLETE ANSWER: Any additional protections could be provided by "smart" firewalls, routers, and switches. Specific commercial devices provide extra defenses:

- **Smart Firewalls.** Smart firewalls include standard protection capabilities. Additionally, firewalls, specifically, can afford whitelisting and blacklisting protections.

- **Whitelisting** is used to allow authorized outside users on an internal Access Control List (ACL). The ACL needs to be managed actively to ensure that legitimate organizations can communicate through the businesses' firewall. The external interested business or organizations can still share with the firm for services like the company website and email system that resides in the Demilitarized Zone (DMZ). Whitelisting is typically implemented at the firewall. See the Diagram below.

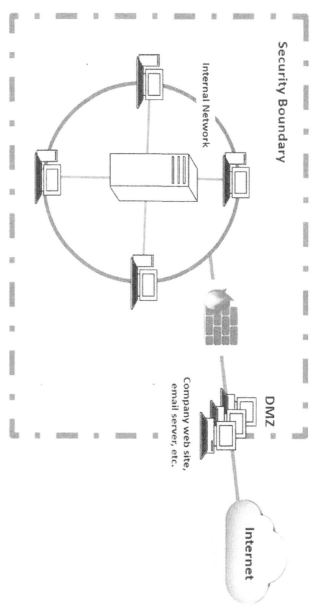

Basic Company Network View

- **Blacklisting** is used to block known "bad guys." Companies and the DOD can provide lists of known malicious sites based upon their Internet addresses. Blacklists require continuous management to be most effective.

These solutions are not guaranteed. While they afford additional means to slow hackers and nation-state intruders, they are not total solutions. Therefore DOD, and much of the cybersecurity community, strongly supports the principle of **Defense in Depth (DID),** where other technological solutions help to reinforce the protections because of security programming flaws inadvertently created by software developers and the constant challenge of hackers exploiting various areas of modern IT architectures to conduct their nefarious actions.

The Principle of Defense in Depth

SI.1.212

3.14.4 Update malicious code protection mechanisms when new releases are available.

MINIMUM/COMPLETE ANSWER: This is usually quickly resolved through software license agreements with vendors for malicious code internal programs or external contracted support services. Assuming a new version is made available during the active period of the license, updates are typically free; document the company's procedure for maintaining not only current but legal versions of malicious code detection and prevention software or services.

SI.1.213

3.14.5 Perform periodic scans of the information system and real-time scans of files from external sources as files are downloaded, opened, or executed.

MINIMUM ANSWER: Solutions afford real-time scanning of files and traffic as they traverse the network. Scanning of files should always be conducted from external downloads for both viruses and malware. Ensure the technical policy settings are always set to perform real-time scans of the network, endpoints (i.e., work computers both internal and used by teleworking employees), and files entering the network using the appropriate tools to ensure network operation and security.

MORE COMPLETE ANSWER: Require IT personnel to regularly check that real-time scanning has not been changed accidentally or on purpose. Manual scans should be done weekly; however, automated alerts are recommended to key cybersecurity staff. It is essential to be aware that potential intruders will attempt to shut down any security features such as active scanning. Train IT personnel to manually check at least weekly and alert management if the changes are suspicious.

LEVEL 2: INTERMEDIATE CYBER HYGIENE

CMMC Certification Controls

55 Security Controls /Total = 72

AC.2.005

3.1.9 Provide privacy and security notices consistent with applicable CUI[9] rules.

MINIMUM ANSWER: Provided below is a current version of the **DOD Warning Banner** designed for company purposes. It should either be physically posted on or near each terminal or on the on-screen logon (preferred); this should also always include consent to monitoring. Recommend consulting with a legal representative for final approval and dissemination to employees.

[Company] Warning Banner[10]

Use of this or any other [Company name] computer system constitutes consent to monitoring at all times.

This is a [Company name] computer system. All [Company name] computer systems and related equipment are intended for the communication, transmission, processing, and storage of official or other authorized information only. All [Company name] computer systems are subject to monitoring at all times to ensure the proper functioning of equipment and systems, including security devices and systems, to prevent unauthorized use and violations of statutes and security regulations, to deter criminal activity, and for other similar purposes. Any user of a [Company name] computer system should be aware that any information placed in the system is subject to monitoring and is not subject to any privacy expectation.

If monitoring of this or any other [Company name] computer system reveals possible evidence of the violation of criminal statutes, this evidence, and any additional related information, including identification information about the user, may be provided to law enforcement officials. If monitoring this or any other [Company name] computer systems reveals violations of security regulations or unauthorized use. These employees who violate security

---

[9] Interpret CUI to mean , FCI, or sensitive information deemed non-releasable to the public.
[10] This warning banner is based upon the DOD's Security Technical Implementation Guide (STIG).

regulations or make unauthorized use of [Company name] computer systems are subject to appropriate disciplinary action.

Use of this or any other [Company name] computer system constitutes consent to monitoring at all times.

MORE COMPLETE ANSWER: Another consideration should be that this policy also is coordinated with Human Resources (HR). This could further include that all employees sign a copy of this notice, and it is placed in their official file. Select and redacted documents could be used to demonstrate an active adherence to this requirement as a sampling provided to DOD. It could also potentially describe how the company can act against personnel who fail or violate this warning.

AC.2.006

3.1.21 Limit use of organizational portable storage devices on external systems.

MINIMUM ANSWER: This is not only about the use of USB thumb drives; it is also about external drives attached to a workstation or laptop locally. While thumb drives are more capable of introducing malware and viruses to an unprotected network, external drives pose a real threat to data removal and theft. The company policy should include an approval process to "attach" only company-provided drives and highly discourage personal devices attached by employees. Technical support should consist of the active scanning for viruses and malware every time the portable device is connected to the network.

MORE COMPLETE ANSWER: As discussed in more detail below regarding the use of thumb drives, IT personnel could disable anyone from using the **registry**. The need for external drives is necessitated. This control can be further enhanced by auditing all such attachments and providing pre-formatted reports for company leadership. Auditing, as described under the AU control, should include capturing this activity.

AC.2.007

3.1.5 Employ the principle of least privilege, including for specific security functions and privileged accounts.

MINIMUM ANSWER: The principle of least privilege is a vital cybersecurity tenet. The least privilege concept is about allowing only authorized access for users and processes that they have direct responsibility. It is limited to only a necessary level of access to accomplish tasks for specific business functions. This should be described in the corporate cybersecurity policy document. This should also be part of basic user agreements to include what is described in DOD terminology, an **Acceptable Use Policy** (AUP).

MORE COMPLETE ANSWER: Much like the controls described above, a sampling of employees' print-outs or screen captures could show selected and authorized individual rights. A sample, especially of privileged users and their assigned roles within the company's IT infrastructure, would target potential third-party DOD assessors. Assessors would use this to support the developing CMMC process.

AC.2.008

3.1.6 Use non-privileged accounts or roles when accessing nonsecurity functions.

MINIMUM ANSWER: It is best to always first answer controls from a policy or procedural solution. Essentially, this is preventing "general users" from accessing the corporate infrastructure and creating accounts, deleting databases, or elevating their privileges to gain access to both CUI/FCI and sensitive corporate data. This is about providing the least amount of access and privilege based upon the duties assigned. Companies will see the control below that mandates a separation not just of responsibilities but access as well based on position and a clear need-to-know.

MORE COMPLETE ANSWER: The more-complete answer could be through automated solutions that monitor access to other security functions such as password resets, account creation, etc. This could include logging and review of all system access. It could also have automated tools that restrict access based upon a user's rights. These technical settings within the tool are established by company policy and monitored by, for example, the local SA.

Auditor, Accreditor, or Assessor?

The correct term is "Assessor." Under RMF, the senior official that reports to the lead risk acceptor, the Authorizing Official (AO), is the Security Control Assessor (SCA). The SCA is typically a government official with a team of government, contractor, or mix of security control assessors. For this reason, the correct term under RMF would be an <u>assessor</u>.

AC.2.009
3.1.8 Limit unsuccessful logon attempts.

MINIMUM ANSWER: DOD standard policy is after **three** failed logins, the system will automatically lock out the individual. Suggest this should be no more than five failed logins, especially if employees are not computer savvy. This requires both the technical solution by the corporate IT system and described in the corporate procedure guide.

MORE COMPLETE ANSWER: For example, the additional ability to provide a screen capture that provides an artifact showing what happens when an employee reaches the maximum number of logons would meet this control; this could be added to the submission packet. It is also essential to document procedures to include the process to regain network access.

AC.2.010
3.1.10. Use session lock with pattern-hiding displays to prevent access/viewing of data after a period of inactivity.

MINIMUM ANSWER: While this may appear as solely a technical solution, it too should be identified in the company policy or procedure document. Session lock describes the period of inactivity when a computer terminal will automatically lock out the user. Suggest no more than 10 minutes for a computer lockout. Selecting longer is acceptable based upon many factors such as the type of work done (e.g., finance personnel) or the business's physical security level (e.g., a restricted area with a limited number of authorized employees) is acceptable. However, be prepared to defend the balance between the company's need to meet DOD mission requirements and the risks of excessive session lock timeouts.

Secondarily, **Pattern Hiding** is desired to prevent the concept of "shoulder surfing." Other like terms that are synonymous include **masking** and **obfuscation**.

> Password without Pattern Hiding: PA$$w0rD
>
> Password with Pattern Hiding:
> ************

Pattern hiding is designed to prevent an individual from observing an employee typing their password or Personal Identification Number (PIN). This control could include asterisks (*), for example, that mask the correct information. This prevents insiders or even visitors from "stealing" another user's login credentials.

MORE COMPLETE ANSWER: The better solution could include much shorter periods for a time-out and longer password length and complexity; the DOD standard is at least 15 alpha-numeric and special characters.

- Alpha: abcde….
- Numeric: 12345…
- Special Characters: @ # $ % ….

As an ongoing reminder, it is critical to place artifacts describing the technical solution demonstrated using "screen capture." It should be clear and easily traceable to this control's implementation by a DOD audit representative or assessor.

AC.2.011

3.1.16 Authorize wireless access prior to allowing such connections.

MINIMUM ANSWER: This would include wireless access agreements and, more commonly described earlier, is an Acceptable Use Policy (AUP). For example, an AUP would define the types and kinds of sites restricted from employees' access. These are typically gambling, pornography sites, etc. A lawyer should review AUP's before requiring employees to sign.

MORE COMPLETE ANSWER: The more-complete technical solution could identify unapproved sites and prevent "guest" access. (While guest access is not recommended, it is better to establish a secondary Wi-Fi network to accommodate and restrict visitors and third-party personnel from having direct access to the company network.)

It is also essential that the Wi-Fi network topology and encryption standard be provided as an artifact to DOD once the final packet is ready for submission. This should be part of the SSP and the corporate cybersecurity procedure document.

AC.2.013

3.1.12 Monitor and control remote access sessions.[11]

MINIMUM ANSWER: This control is about remote access where one computer can control another computer over the Internet. This may include desktop support personnel "remoting into" an employee's computer to update the latest version of Firefox ® or a work-at-home employee inputting financial data into the corporate finance system. Identify these types of access as part of the procedural guide and describe who is authorized, how their access is limited (such as a finance employee cannot issue themselves a corporate check), and the repercussions of violating the policy.

MORE COMPLETE ANSWER: The better technological approach could include restrictions to only IT help personnel using remote capabilities. Company policy should require regular review of auditable events and logs. A screen capture would be helpful to show the policy settings specific to the remote desktop application.

---

[11] This control may be tailored out if remote access or maintenance is not allowed.

AC.2.015

3.1.14 Route remote access[12] via managed access control points.

MINIMUM ANSWER: Managed access control points are about control of traffic through "trusted" connections. For example, Verizon ® or AT&T® as the company's Internet Service Provider (ISP). It would be highly recommended to include any contracted services or Service Level Agreements (SLA)[13] from these providers. They may consist of additional threat and spam filtering services that could reduce the "bad guys" from gaining access to corporate data; these are ideal artifacts for proof of satisfactorily meeting this control.

MORE COMPLETE ANSWER: Another addition could also be using a **Virtual Private Network (VPN).** These are also common services the significant providers have for additional costs.

Describing and providing such agreements to DOD could also identify a **defense in depth** approach; the first level is through the VPN service. The second would be provided by the remote access software providing an additional layer of defense. Defense in depth can include such protective efforts to prevent unauthorized access to company IT assets:

- Physical protection (e.g., alarms, guards)
- Perimeter (e.g., firewalls, Intrusion Detection System (IDS), "Trusted Internet Connections")
- Application/Executables (e.g., **whitelisting** of authorized software, **blacklisting** blocking specified programs)
- Data (e.g., Data Loss Protection programs, Access controls, auditing).

AC.2.016

3.1.3 Control the flow of CUI flowing the approved authorizations.

MINIMUM ANSWER: Companies typically use **flow control** policies and technologies to manage the movement of CUI/FCI throughout the IT architecture; flow control is based on the types of information.

In terms of procedural updates, discussion of the corporate documents should address several areas of concern: 1) That only authorized personnel within the

---

[12] Reminder, if you are not allowing for remote access, specify that the control is NA for that reason.

[13] See the latest version of **"The Cloud Service Level Agreement (CSLA): A Supplement for NIST 800-171 Implementation"** on Amazon for more information about the CSLA when seeking to deploy part or all of the corporate IT environment with a Cloud Service Provider (CSP).

company with the requisite need-to-know are provided access; 2) appropriate security measures are in place to include encryption while Data is in Transit (DIT); 3) what are the procedures for handling internal employees who violate these company rules? 4) how does the company alert DOD if there is external access (hackers) to its IT infrastructure and its CUI/FCI?

MORE COMPLETE ANSWER: Addressing this control can further be demonstrated by implementing training as a form of **mitigation**; mitigation are other supporting efforts, not just technical, that can reduce the effects of a threat that exploits this control. The company could also include risk from insider threats (See Control 3.2.3 for discussion of "insider threat.") by requiring employees to complete Non-disclosure (NDA) and non-compete agreements (NCA). These added measures *reduce or mitigate the risk to the IT infrastructure*. They should also address employees that depart, resign, or are terminated by the company; the consideration is for disgruntled employees that may leave the company with potentially sensitive CUI/FCI.

Flow control could also be better shown to a DOD assessor in terms of a technical solution. This could be further demonstrated by using encryption for DIT and Data at Rest (DAR). These encryption requirements within the CMMC necessitate differing technical solutions and Federal Information Processing Standards (FIPS) 140-2 compliance; see Control 3.13.11 for more details.

The answer could also include weekly reviews of access logs. Typically, IT support personnel or the SA would conduct recurring audits. If anomalies are detected, what is the procedure to alert senior management to staff attempting access to CUI/FCI and other sensitive data? This offers a more significant demonstration of company security measures to DOD representatives.

EXAMPLE PROCEDURE: "The ABC IT System application restricts transactions and functions. All users will abide by these restrictions based upon their duty position and role(s). Furthermore, procedural implementation requires personnel to read and accept their responsibilities under the company's Acceptable Use Policy (AUP) (See Annex A). Users and privileged users will be limited to only those transactions and functions required to accomplish their mission.

The Company Employs Defense in Depth (DID) as the basis of all security measures. It begins with security and awareness

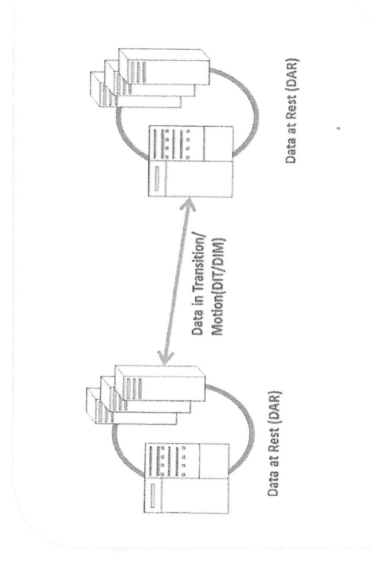

**Data at Rest (DAR) versus Data in Transit/Motion (DIT/DIM)
Conceptual Diagram**

AU.2.041

3.3.2 Ensure that the actions of individual information system users can be uniquely traced to those users, so they can be held accountable for their actions.

MINIMUM ANSWER: This is about the capture of individual users as they access the system. Access logs should include, for example, user identification information, timestamps of all access, databases or applications accessed, and some failed login attempts. This control is designed for potential forensic reconstruction for either internal policy violations or external threat intrusions. Any policy considerations should include at least a weekly review, but any audit review periodicity should be based on data sensitivity and criticality to the business's overall mission.

MORE COMPLETE ANSWER: A more complete means to address this control is using automated alerts to crucial IT and management personnel. This could include capabilities from existing "smart" firewalls, or more advanced solutions may consist of a **Security Information & Event Management** (SIEM) solution. These are more complicated and expensive solutions, but current developments employing modern Artificial Intelligence and Machine Learning technologies to identify threats evolve rapidly and proactively; these solutions should be less costly and more comfortable to deploy within the next decade.

Synopsis of the Audit and Accountability Control Family

The Audit (AU) control is primarily about the system owner/company's ability to monitor unauthorized access to the system through system logging functions of the Operating System and other network devices such as firewalls. A System Administrator (SA) is typically assigned to review log files; these may include both authorized and unauthorized access to the network, applications, databases, financial systems, etc. Most businesses will rely on manual review; however, some "smart" servers and firewalls can provide automated alerts to IT personnel of unauthorized use or intrusion. The key is to understand the corporate system's auditing capabilities and be prepared to defend its capabilities and limitations if DOD representatives or third-party DOD assessors request proof of control compliance.

```
...sion Detection System

.[**] [1:1407:9] SNMP trap udp [**]
[Classification: Attempted Information Leak] [Priority: 2]
03/06-8:14:09.082119 192.168.1.167:1052 -> 172.30.128.27:162
UDP TTL:118 TOS:0x0 ID:29101 IpLen:20 DgmLen:87
```

Personal Firewall

```
3/6/2006 8:14:07 AM,"Rule ""Block Windows File Sharing"" blocked (192.168.1.54,
netbios-ssn(139)).","Rule ""Block Windows File Sharing"" blocked (192.168.1.54,
netbios-ssn(139)). Inbound TCP connection. Local address,service is
(KENT(172.30.128.27),netbios-ssn(139)). Remote address,service is
(192.168.1.54,39922). Process name is ""System""."

3/3/2006 9:04:04 AM,Firewall configuration updated: 398 rules.,Firewall configuration
updated: 398 rules.
```

Antivirus Software, Log 1

```
3/4/2006 9:33:50 AM,Definition File Download,KENT,userk,Definition downloader
3/4/2006 9:33:09 AM,AntiVirus Startup,KENT,userk,System
3/3/2006 3:56:46 PM,AntiVirus Shutdown,KENT,userk,System
```

Antivirus Software, Log 2

```
240203071234,16,3,7,KENT,userk,.....,16777216,"Virus definitions are
current.",0,,0,,,,,0,.........SAVPROD,{ xxxxxxxx-xxxx-xxxx-xxxx-xxxxxxxxxxxx },End
User,{IP}-192.168.1.121,,GROUP,0:0:0:0:0:0,9.0.0.338,.............
```

Antispyware Software

```
DSO Exploit: Data source object exploit (Registry change, nothing done)  HKEY_USERS\S-
1-5-19\Software\Microsoft\Windows\CurrentVersion\Internet_Settings\Zones\0\1004!=W=³
```

Audit log type examples. The logs above are good examples of the system logs that should be reviewed regularly. These are the business's responsibility to monitor the network actively. Another high-interest term is **Continuous Monitoring (ConMon);** see the article in **Appendix C** discussing the importance of ConMon capabilities. Both manual and automated means can accomplish ConMon, and auditing is a significant control family supporting this cybersecurity principle's objectives.

ConMon activities are best described as the business's ability to "continuously" monitor the state of its network within its defined security boundary. It should be a capability to determine, for example, who, when, and what are within the company's security boundary and any reporting requirements in the event of an intrusion. It will be based on the log discovery of unauthorized activities. (SOURCE: *Guide to Computer Security Log Management*, NIST SP 800-92, September 2006, http://nvlpubs.nist.gov/nistpubs/Legacy/SP/nistspecialpublication800-92.pdf) .

AU.2.042

3.3.1 Create, protect, and retain information system audit records to the extent needed to enable the monitoring, analysis, investigation, and reporting of unlawful, unauthorized, or inappropriate information system activity.

MINIMUM ANSWER: The critical part of this control is about audit record retention. The control defines the retention period as a vague capability to retain such records to the most significant "extent possible." The guidance should always be based on the sensitivity of the data. Another consideration should include providing forensic data to investigators to determine the intrusion over a period.

The historical OPM Breach occurred over several years until OPM even recognized multiple incidents. This included the exfiltration of millions of personnel and security background investigation files. While many, including poor audit processes and review, OPM failures are a significant factor in the success of nation-state hackers. OPM's flawed audit and retention processes made reconstructing critical events more than difficult for government forensics and associated criminal investigations.

The recommendation to small and medium businesses conducting DOD contract activities would be at least one year and preferably two years of audit log retention. Companies should regularly discuss with DOD its specified requirements and should also visit the National Archives Record Agency (NARA) (www.nara.gov) for CUI//FCI data retention as part of an active audit program.

Businesses should always balance operations (and long-term costs) with security (the ability to reconstruct an intrusion, to support law enforcement)

MORE COMPLETE ANSWER: A greater ability to recognize breaches (events and incidents) could include a new internal process and assigned first-responders who would act upon these occurrences. This response team may have additional specialized training to include the use of select network analysis support tools to include packet inspection training using tools such as Wireshark ® (https://www.wireshark.org/).

AU.2.043

3.3.7 Provide an information system capability that compares and synchronizes internal system clocks with an authoritative source to generate timestamps for audit records.

MINIMUM ANSWER: The most straightforward answer is to have IT personnel use the Network Time Protocol (NTP) on **NTP port 123** to provide US Naval Observatory timestamps as the network's standard. This is used as the authoritative source within DOD. The system clocks of all processors (computers, firewalls, etc.) within the company should be set to the same time when first initialized by IT support staff; this should be an explicit policy requirement.

It is suggested that SA personnel review and compare the external (NTP server time stamp) with internal system clocks. This can be used to identify log changes if synchronization is not the same from the external and internal clock settings. Log changes may be an indicator of unauthorized access and manipulation of log files by hackers.

MORE COMPLETE ANSWER: Several automated programs can be used, and good basic programmers within the company could write scripts (small pieces of executable code) to provide these comparisons more easily.

AU.2.044

AU.2.044: Review and manage audit logs.

MINIMUM ANSWER: Address this control in the cybersecurity policy. Suppose there are no automated alerts built into local security devices. SAs should be checking the logs, operating system, network system, and anti-virus logs at least weekly. The policy should identify the reporting process for notifying local IT professionals to include the companies CIO or CISO. This should also address its relationship with incident response and reporting criteria.

MORE COMPLETE ANSWER: If there are automated capabilities to alert on-call IT professionals, this should be addressed as either near or real-time notifications and responses to the IT and cybersecurity designated staff. This portion of the policy should also include the designation of all automated security solutions, including smart firewalls and Security Incident Event Managers (SIEM).

AT.2.056

3.2.1 Ensure that managers, systems administrators, and users of organizational information systems are made aware of the security risks associated with their activities and of the applicable policies, standards, and procedures related to the security of organizational information systems.

MINIMUM ANSWER: Human beings are the weakest link in the cybersecurity "war." The greatest threat is from the employee who unwittingly selects a link that allows an intrusion into the corporate system, or worse, those who maliciously remove, modify or delete sensitive CUI/FCI.

The answer should be documented regarding initial and annual refresher training requirements for everyone in the company, not average employees but must include senior managers and support subcontractors. Provide a sampling of select employees that have taken the training and ensuring it is current within the past year.

MORE COMPLETE ANSWER: A possible demonstration of the more-complete solution is within the policy-specific direction to IT support personnel. There could be a system notification that allows them, after notice, manually or by automated means, to suspend access to training is completed. Substantial documentation is important specific to awareness training.

Synopsis of Cybersecurity Awareness & Training

Cybersecurity Awareness & Training (AT-control) is about an active cybersecurity training program for employees and a regular education program that consistently ensures their familiarity and compliance with protecting sensitive and CUI/FCI company data. The websites (below) identify FREE government-sponsored sites a company can leverage without expending any of its resources. The three major training requirements that can be expected of most vendors supporting federal government contract activities include:

1. **Cybersecurity Awareness Training.**
   https://securityawareness.usalearning.gov/cybersecurity/index.htm

2. **Insider Threat Training.**
   https://securityawareness.usalearning.gov/itawareness/index.htm
   (More discussion on the "Insider Threat" topic See Control 3.2.3).

3. **Privacy.** https://iatraining.disa.mil/eta/piiv2/launchPage.htm (This would correctly apply to any company that handles, processes, or maintains Personally Identifiable Information (PII) and Personal Health Information (PHI). The author expects that even though a company does not handle PII or PHI, the federal government will direct this as a universal training requirement.)

Defense Security Service (DSS) Cybersecurity Awareness Site

AT.2.057

3.2.2 Ensure that organizational personnel are adequately trained to carry out their assigned information, security-related duties and responsibilities.

MINIMUM ANSWER: This is required not only awareness training but also specialized training for privileged users. This is usually an Operating System (OS) training specific to the company's architecture. It is possible to have multiple OSs. Privileged users are only required to show, for example, some form of the training certificate to meet this requirement. All IT personnel who have elevated privileges must have such training before they are authorized to execute their duties.

Additionally, if the company uses Microsoft ® or Linux ® Operating Systems, privileged users will have some certification level to show familiarity with these programs. This could include major national certifications for these applications or introductory familiarity courses from free training sites, for example, Khan Academy® (https://www.khanacademy.org/) or Udacity® (https://www.udacity.com/).

DOD has not defined the level and type of training for this requirement. It requires privileged users to understand and train certificates (with no specified time length) for the dominant Operating System (OS) the corporate IT infrastructure employs.

MORE COMPLETE ANSWER: If IT personnel have formal certification (such as from a Microsoft ® partner training program), these are ideal artifacts that should be part of the BOE.

CM.2.061

3.4.1 Establish and maintain baseline configurations and inventories of organizational information systems (including hardware, software, firmware, and documentation) throughout the respective system development life cycles.

MINIMUM ANSWER: This control can be best met by hardware, software, and firmware (should be combined with hardware) listings; these are the classic artifacts required for any system within the DOD. Updating these documents as changes to the IT architecture is both a critical IT and logistics' function. Ensure these staffs are well-coordinated about system changes. ***This should be included in the System Security Plan (SSP).***

Also, the CMMC requires document control of all reports, documents, manuals, etc. The currency of all related documents should be managed in a centralized repository.

Where documents may be sensitive, such as describing existing weaknesses or vulnerabilities of the IT infrastructure, these documents should have a higher control level. The rationale for greater control of such materials is if these documents were "found" in the public, hackers, or Advanced Persistent Threats (i.e., adversarial nation-states) could use this information to conduct exploits. Vulnerabilities about company systems should be marked and controlled, at least at the CUI/FCI level.

MORE COMPLETE ANSWER: Suggested better approaches to exercising good **version control** activities would be using a shared network drive, or a more advanced solution could use Microsoft ® SharePoint ®. An active version control tool should only allow authorized personnel to make changes to critical documents and system changes and their associated **versioning**—significant changes within the IT architecture, such as version 2.0 to 3.0. This should also maintain audit records of who and when a file is accessed and modified.

A Synopsis of the True Foundation of Cybersecurity

The real importance of Configuration Management is it is, in fact, the "opposite side of the same coin" called cybersecurity. CM is used to track and confirm changes to the system's baseline; this could be changed in hardware, firmware, and software that would alert IT professionals to unauthorized modifications to the IT environment. CM is used to confirm and ensure programmatic controls prevent changes that have not been adequately tested or approved.

CM requires establishing baselines for tracking, controlling, and managing a business's internal IT infrastructure specific to the CMMC. Companies with an effective CM process need to consider information security implications for information systems' development and operation.

This will include the active management of changes to company hardware, software, and documentation.

Effective CM of information systems requires the integration of the management of secure configurations into the CM process. If good CM exists as a well-defined "change" process, the IT environment's protection is more assured. This should be considered as the second most important security control. It is suggested that both management and IT personnel have adequate knowledge and training to maintain this process since it is integral to good programmatic and cybersecurity practice.

CM.2.062

3.4.6 Employ the principle of least functionality by configuring the information system to provide only essential capabilities.

MINIMUM ANSWER: The DOD has defined the use, for example, of File Transfer Protocol (FTP), Bluetooth, or peer-to-peer networking as insecure protocols. These protocols are unauthorized within DOD environments, and companies seeking CMMC approval are best to follow this direction as well. Any written procedure should attempt to at least annually reassess whether a determination of the security of all functions, ports, protocols, or services is still correct.

MORE COMPLETE ANSWER: The use of automated network packet tools is recommended to conduct such reassessments. Ensure that IT personnel have the right experience and skill to analyze this control requirement properly.

CM.2.063

3.4.9 Control and monitor user-installed software.

MINIMUM ANSWER: The policy should always be that only authorized administrators, such as designated SA's and senior help desk personnel, be allowed to add or delete the software from user computers.

There should also be a defined process to request specialized software to be added for unique users. These may include finance personnel, architects, statisticians, etc. that require specialized stand-alone software that may or may not connect to the Internet.

MORE COMPLETE ANSWER: This could include the review of whether personnel is adding software and bypassing security measures (such as getting passwords from IT authorized individuals) as part of the company's normal audit process. This may also be addressed in the AUP and supported by appropriate HR activities that can be pursued against individuals of any such violations.

CM.2.064

3.4.2 Establish and enforce security configuration settings for information technology products employed in organizational information systems.

MINIMUM/MORE COMPLETE ANSWER: There should be an identification of any security configuration settings in the business's procedural documents. This would include technical policy settings, for example, the number of failed logins, minimum password length, mandatory logoff settings, etc. These settings should be identified by a company's Operating System, software application, or program.

EXAMPLE PROCEDURE: "The company's privileged users will support the CM process and its implementation per DODI 5000.02, Enclosure 12-5, NIST-SP 800-128, and STIGS for all hardware and software components (https://public.cyber.mil/stigs/). This includes establishing CM levels to maintain the accredited security posture following all implemented security controls. The established Configuration Control Board (CCB) will generally include users, programmers, system engineers, system administrators, and cybersecurity personnel to provide diverse expertise of system and system security lifecycle actions."

CM.2.065

3.4.3 Track, review, approve/disapprove, and audit changes to information systems.

MINIMUM ANSWER: This control addresses a defined corporate change *process*. This should add or remove IT components within the network and provide needed currency regarding the state of the system. This should not be a purely IT staff function. If the firm can afford additional infrastructure personnel, it should assign a configuration manager to administer the CM process.

MORE COMPLETE ANSWER: This could use Commercial Off the Shelf Technologies (COTS) that could be used to establish a more sophisticated CM database. This could also afford a more capable audit ability to prevent unauthorized changes.

CM.2.066

3.4.4 Analyze the security impact of changes prior to implementation.

MINIMUM ANSWER: Under DOD's risk management process, it requires that any changes to the baseline necessitate some level of technical analysis. This analysis is described as a **Security Impact Analysis (SIA),** and it is looking for any positive or negative changes that are considered **security-relevant**.

This analysis should look at any change to the architecture, be it hardware, software, firmware, or architecture. This should be described in the corporate CM process and could be as basic as a write-up from a member of the IT team, for example, the change will or will not have a security impact, and it may or may not be security-relevant.

Suppose the change introduces a "negative" impact, such as eliminating backup capabilities or adding currently unsupportable software (possibly due to funding constraints). In that case, ***it is the company's responsibility*** *to reinitiate the CMMC process in-full and advise DOD of the rationale for the change.*

MORE COMPLETE ANSWER: A more-complete solution to this control would include, for example, the addition of a new software product that supports vulnerability scans using corporate anti-virus and malware applications or software products. Attach these reports as part of the record.

In the case of hardware updates, the company could demonstrate its SCRM process by attaching proof that the manufacturer is an authorized vendor approved by the DOD. Access to DOD's Approved Products List (APL) may require the Contracting Officer Representative (COR) or Contracting Officer (CO) to approve access to DOD databases maintained by the Defense Information Systems Agency (DISA) at Fort Meade, MD. It most likely will only allow a limited number of company personnel to be issued DOD CAC "tokens" to access these sites; the positive review of these databases will demonstrate the proper level of due diligence for any current or future Authorization to Operate (ATO).

IA.2.078

3.5.7 Enforce a minimum password complexity and change of characters when new passwords are created.

MINIMUM ANSWER: If using passwords for authentication purposes, the expectation is that a POAM has been developed until such time a 2FA or MFA solution is in place. The standard complexity is supposed to be at least 15 characters that include at least two or more alpha, numeric, and special characters to reduce the likelihood of compromise. (See Appendix D: *Managing the Lifecycle of a POAM*).

MORE COMPLETE ANSWER: Automated policy settings of the network can enforce increased length and variability. Another suggestion is to use passphrases. These can be harder to "crack" by standard hacking tools and are typically easier for users to memorize.

EXAMPLE PROCEDURE: "Passwords are an essential aspect of our security. A poor password may result in unauthorized access or exploitation of resources. All users, including contractors and vendors with access to systems, are responsible for taking the appropriate steps to select and secure their passwords.

All COMPANY personnel will abide by the *Company's Password Policy.* This policy enhances those requirements to include:

- All user-level and system-level passwords must be at least 14 characters with alphanumeric and symbols. At least two characters will be used from all three categories: alphabetical, numerical, and special character, respectively, IAW Windows Server® 16 STIG.
- Users must not use the same password for the account for other non-access (for example, personal email account, bank account, etc.).
- Passwords may not be reused for at 24 iterations of password changes IAW applicable STIG."

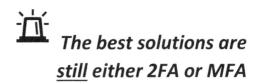

The best solutions are <u>still</u> either 2FA or MFA

The factors:

1. Something you know (e.g., password/PIN)
2. Something you have (e.g., cryptographic identification device, token)
3. Something you are (e.g., biometric: fingerprint, iris, etc.).

IA.2.079

3.5.8 Prohibit password reuse for a specified number of generations.
MINIMUM ANSWER: This is usually set by policy and the designated SA's that limit the number of times a password can be reused; **passwords within DOD are required to be changed every 90 days.** This function should be automated by authorized IT personnel. The suggested reuse of a prior password should be at least ten or higher. Confirm current requirements with the KO/Co for the contract.

MORE COMPLETE ANSWER: Technical settings can be established for **no** reuse. This ensures that hackers who may have exploited one of the user's other businesses or even (and more especially) personal accounts can be less likely to be effective against corporate computer networks and assets.

IA.2.080

3.5.9 Allow temporary password use for system logons with an immediate change to a permanent password.
MINIMUM/MORE COMPLETE ANSWER: This setting is typically built into standard network operating systems. This requirement for users should be appropriately included in the recommended procedure guide.

IA.2.081

3.5.10 Store and transmit an only encrypted representation of passwords.

MINIMUM ANSWER: This is both a DIT and DAR issue. See Control 3.1.3 for a conceptual diagram. IT personnel should be regularly verifying that password data stores are always encrypted.

This control requires that all passwords are encrypted and approved by NIST's sanctioned process under FIPS 140-2. See Control 3.13.11 for the NIST website to confirm whether a cryptographic solution is approved.

MORE COMPLETE ANSWER: Suggested greater protections could require encrypted passwords that are not collocated on the same main application or database server that stores significant portions of the business's data repository. A separate server (physical or virtual) could prevent hackers from exploits from accessing company data stores.

IA.2.082

3.5.11. Obscure feedback of authentication information.

MINIMUM/MORE COMPLETE ANSWER: This is like **pattern hiding,** as described in Control 3.1.10. The system should prevent unauthorized individuals from compromising system-level authentication by inadvertently observing in-person ("shoulder surfing") or virtually (by viewing password entries by privileged users) remotely. It relies upon obscuring the "feedback of authentication information," for example, displaying asterisks (*) or hash symbols (#) when a user types their password. This setting should be enforced automatically and prevent general users from changing this setting.

IR.2.092

3.6.1 Establish an operational incident-handling capability for organizational information systems that includes adequate preparation, detection, analysis, containment, recovery, and user response activities.

MINIMUM ANSWER: This control addresses a "capability" that needs to be established to respond to events and incidents within the firm's IT security boundary.

This should include the **People, Process, and Technology (PPT) Model** as a recommended guide for answering many of the controls within CMMC. While solutions will not necessarily require a technological answer, consideration of the people (e.g., who? what skill sets? etc.) and process (e.g., notifications to senior management, action workflows, etc.) will meet many of the response requirements.

Use the Cyber Incident **Life Cycle** above to guide the company's operational incident-handling artifact/procedure. This should be an annex to the **SSP**. The PPT Model can be used to guide and formulate the IRP annex. A suggested approach is described below and includes the kinds of questions that should be answered to demonstrate best how best to develop a good IRP:

- Preparation
    - People: Who will perform the action or activity? Training needed? Skill sets?
    - Process: Training policies for cybersecurity and IT professionals to support the IRP
    - Technology: What technology already exists to support IR? What techniques are needed?

- Detection
    - People: Are IT staff able to use audit tools properly to detect intrusions?
    - Process: What are 'best practice' approaches to detect intrusions? Monitor firewall logs? Monitor user activity?

- Technology: Is the technology's data library current? Are automatic updates enabled?

- Analysis
  - People: Are IT staff capable of doing the analysis required? Can they determine false positive activity?
  - Process: What is the process leadership wants to get useful and actionable data from IT staff? What are the demands for immediate and final reporting timelines?
  - Technology: Are the right tools on-site? Can open-source/web solutions useful? Can DOD or DHS provide valuable data feeds to remain current on threats?

- Containment
  - People: Can IT staff stop the ongoing attack? Do they require additional coding scripting skills to build/update firewall policies?
  - Process: Is the containment process effective? Is allowing the attack to continue identifying the threat entity/location a good idea (to support law enforcement)?
  - Technology: Can software tools quarantine and stop a malware attack? Is shutting down all external connections an excellent immediate solution (at the firewall)?

- Recovery Actions
  - People: Can the IT staff recover backup data files and media?
  - Process: What is the order of recovery? Bring up internal databases and communications first, and external servers (email and website) be reestablished later? What are the recovery time standards for the company to regain business operations? What is acceptable? What is not sufficient?
  - Technology: Are there adequate numbers of backup devices for critical systems? Can third-party service providers assist in recovering lost or damaged data?

- User Response Activities
  - People: Can employees safely return to an operational state?

- Process: Does the company need to control access to services to select individuals first (e.g., finance, logistics, etc.)
- Technology: Can technology resolve immediate problems from the recovery vice the employee such as, for example, reselecting printers and other data connections?

MORE COMPLETE ANSWER: In those situations, when control is specifically discussing a policy solution, the employment of automated tools, alerts, etc., should always be considered. Even the use of essential tracking tools such as Microsoft ® Excel ® and Access ® will demonstrate a level of positive control over the IT environment.

What do you do when you are attacked?

The Incident Response (IR) control family primarily requires a plan, identifying who or what agency is notified when a breach has occurred and testing of that plan over time. This control requires the development of an Incident Response Plan (IRP). There are many templates available online, and if there is an existing relationship with a DOD agency, companies should be able to get an agency-specific template.

OCCURRENCE →

EVENT (initial observation of potential problem) →

INCIDENT (defined/confirmed/high impact)

Incident Response Spectrum

The first effort should be identifying with DOD representatives what constitutes a reportable event that formally becomes an incident. This could include a confirmed breach that has occurred to the IT infrastructure. Incidents could contain anything from a Denial of Service

(DOS) attack—overloading of outwardly facing web or mail servers--or exfiltration of data—where CUI/FCI and corporate data has been copied or moved to outside of the company's firewall/perimeter. Incidents could also include the destruction of data that the company's IT staff, for example, identifies through ongoing audit activities.

Secondarily, who do you notify? Do you alert your assigned Contract Officer Representative (COR), the Contract Office, DOD's US Cybercommand at Fort Meade, MD, or possibly the Department of Homeland Security's (DHS) Computer Emergency Response Team (CERT) (https://www.us-cert.gov/forms/report)? Company representatives will have to ask their assigned COR where to file standard DOD "incident" reports. They should be able to provide templates and forms specific to the DOD agency.

Finally, this security control will require testing at least *annually*, but more often is recommended. Until comfortable with the IR "reporting chain," *practice, practice, practice*.

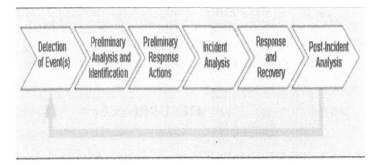

Cyber Incident Life Cycle. This diagram will assist in approaching the IR activity and better assist in coordination with DOD cybersecurity incident response organizations. Recognizing this as either an "event" (not necessarily a negative occurrence) versus an "incident" is an internal call by the company's leadership in coordination with its security and IT professional staff. An incident specifically requires alerting DOD as soon as the intrusion is *recognized*.

Verify with the respective DOD agency its reporting standards. Typically, **events** need to be reported within 24 hours upon recognition and **incidents** immediately upon recognition. Always verify this with the assigned COR.

The chart below categorizes the current DOD precedence and should be used as the basis of triaging multiple attacks.

Precedence	Category	Description
0	0	Training and Exercises
1	1	Root Level Intrusion (Incident)
2	2	User Level Intrusion (Incident)
3	4	Denial of Service (Incident)
4	7	Malicious Logic (Incident)
5	3	Unsuccessful Activity Attempt (Event)
6	5	Non-Compliance Activity (Event)
7	6	Reconnaissance (Event)
8	8	Investigating (Event)
9	9	Explained Anomaly (Event)

DOD Precedence Categorization. Nine (9) is the lowest event where little is known, and IT personnel are attempting to determine whether this activity should be elevated to alert company leadership or to "close it out." One (1) is a deep attack. It identifies that the incident has gained "root" access. This incident level is critical since an intruder has nearly unlimited access to the network and its data. (SOURCE: CYBER INCIDENT HANDLING PROGRAM, CJCSM 6510.01B, 18 December 2014, http://www.jcs.mil/Portals/36/Documents/Library/Manuals/m651001.pdf?ver=2016-02-05-175710-897)

IR.2.093
(CMMC-specific and derived from the CERT RMM Framework)[14]

IR.2.093: Detect and report events.

MINIMUM ANSWER: Identify the most effective methods for event detection. This is company-dependent. As described earlier, a manual review of audit and event logs is allowed; however, these are less effective and more susceptible to failing to detect threats. Automated systems to include "smart" firewalls and SIEM solutions are excellent initial solutions and may also use third-party Security as a Service (Sec-aaS) option. The answer should be identified and documented in the local cybersecurity policy.

MORE COMPLETE ANSWER: Highly recommend the use of the DOD precedence categorization as defined above. The process for reporting events should be provided by the KO/CO via the contract question portion of the solicitation process—press the KO to find the answers. Questions you should ask should include:
- What are the reporting thresholds/timelines for both events and incidents?
- What office agency do you report the information?
- What is the contact information, phone numbers, email addresses, etc., required?
- What passcodes are required to verify your company or agency to the incident repose organization?

Also, assign IT [operational] and cyber-staff [security/oversight] personnel to monitor organizational processes. Remember to employ two-person integrity procedures to prevent insider threat exploits. The organization's System, Database, and Network Administrators are the front line for collecting event data and NOT the Help Desk!

---

[14] The CERT® Resilience Management Model, Version 1.2, February 2016, can be found at https://resources.sei.cmu.edu/asset_files/Handbook/2016_002_001_514462.pdf

IR.2.094
(CMMC-specific; CERT RMM Framework)

IR.2.094: Analyze and triage events to support event resolution and incident declaration.

MINIMUM ANSWER: *Occurrences → lead to events → that lead to incidents.* Incidents are the highest level of threat. Any triage approach should follow the DOD precedence model. Precedence 1 being the most elevated threat and 0 the lowest. This should be part of its Incident Response (IR) portion of its cybersecurity policy and the formal IR Plan (IRP). Where multiple attacks occur of the same precedence, they should be addressed *first-in, first-out (FIFO).* The assumption is the longer a threat is within the local IT environment, the higher the likelihood of damage that will result.

Precedence	Category	Description
0	0	Training and Exercises
1	1	Root Level Intrusion (Incident)
2	2	User Level Intrusion (Incident)
3	4	Denial of Service (Incident)
4	7	Malicious Logic (Incident)
5	3	Unsuccessful Activity Attempt (Event)
6	5	Non-Compliance Activity (Event)
7	6	Reconnaissance (Event)
8	8	Investigating (Event)
9	9	Explained Anomaly (Event)

MORE COMPLETE ANSWER: The IRP should be developed in a more mature security environment. Not all companies will be able to create or respond to threats, but it should be an objective consideration for the organization. An IRP should identify roles and responsibilities and process flows to meeting to cyber-threats. The IRP should also include notifications to DOD, higher headquarters, and customers. The IRP is the foundation of incident response.

IR.2.096
(CMMC-specific; CERT RMM Framework)

IR.2.096: Develop and implement responses to declared incidents according to pre-defined procedures.

MINIMUM ANSWER: Know who or what agency should be notified when an event or incident occurs. The KO/CO should provide minimum thresholds for reporting to DOD and others within the federal government.

MORE COMPLETE ANSWER: As part of the IRP, there are three primary response regimens:
1. **Identify and monitor:** This is passive monitoring of low-level threats and is used as an interim solution until the danger has ceased or elevated its assault. The two answers below should be considered when determining an event becomes a formal incident, as defined in the DOD precedence model described above.
2. **Mitigate/reduce the impacts of attacks.** Consideration should include how and when to isolate portions of the network or de-activation of attack ports or protocols by cyber-threats.
3. **Stop the attack:** A *kill-switch concept* is a radical approach that considers shutting off external connectivity to include firewalls or Internet services. This should only be used in extreme threat scenarios, and senior IT management needs to provide a final determination.

IR.2.097
(CMMC-specific; CERT RMM Framework)

IR.2.097: Perform root cause analysis on incidents to determine underlying causes.

MINIMUM ANSWER/ MORE COMPLETE ANSWER: Root cause analysis should be conducted by designated cybersecurity professional. This may include a forensics specialist, System administrator, information security officer, or Chief Information Security Officer (CISO). The cybersecurity policy should select a primary and alternate to conduct incident root cause analysis.

MA.2.111
3.7.1 Perform maintenance on organizational information systems.

MINIMUM ANSWER: This should describe the company's maintenance procedures for its IT infrastructure. This could include either internal maintenance teams or third-party companies. This will consist of hardware component repairs and replacements, printer repairs, etc. Any maintenance agreements should be provided as artifacts to support an authorization package.

MORE COMPLETE ANSWER: Maintenance could include identifying computer hardware spares on-site or at company warehouse locations. The company's logistics personnel should manage operational spares; they should be captured within the property book database and its associated hard copy reporting to senior management.

EXAMPLE PROCEDURE: "COMPANY software developer accomplishes software code maintenance to include the creation and updating of application code. Hardware maintenance is provided by network and logistics personnel. They will provide or coordinate fixes, replacements, or third-party maintainers. Furthermore, all software and hardware warranty services are administered by Company IT Operations Division. The Program Manager has overall responsibility for ensuring maintenance activities are timely, prompt, and complete."

MA.2.112

3.7.2 Provide effective controls on the tools, techniques, mechanisms, and personnel used to conduct information system maintenance.

MINIMUM ANSWER: This control relates to tools used for diagnostics and repairs of the company's IT system/network. These tools include, for example, hardware/software diagnostic test equipment and hardware/software **packet sniffers**. Access to the hardware tools should be secured in lockable containers and only accessed by authorized IT personnel.

In software tools, they should be restricted to personnel with privileged user rights and specifically audited when any user is required or needed.

MORE COMPLETE ANSWER: Suggested additional control may include two-person integrity requirements. This would require that when any of these tools are utilized, at least two authorized individuals are involved in any system maintenance or diagnostic activities.

MA.2.113

3.7.5 Require multifactor authentication to establish nonlocal maintenance sessions via external network connections and terminate such connections when nonlocal maintenance is complete.

MINIMUM ANSWER: Nonlocal maintenance is those diagnostic or repair activities conducted over network communications to include the Internet or dedicated least circuits.

This requires that any external third-party maintenance activities use some form of Multi-Factor Authentication (MFA) to access company IT hardware and software components directly. If IT personnel working with outside maintainers can use an MFA solution, they most likely have a robust IT support capability. If not, then this control is a good candidate for an early POAM; ensure good milestones are established for monthly review, for example, "on-going research," "market survey of potential candidate solutions," "identification of funding sources," etc.

MORE COMPLETE ANSWER: A complete answer requires a technical solution. As discussed earlier, the use of CAC, PIV cards, or tokens, such as the RSA ® rotating encryption keying devices, are ideal solutions. This solution most likely will require additional analysis and funding approaches to select the most appropriate answer.

MA.2.114

3.7.6 Supervise the maintenance activities of maintenance personnel without required access authorization.

MINIMUM ANSWER: The procedure requirement should reflect that non-company maintenance personnel should always be escorted. An access log should be maintained, and it should include, for example, the individual or individuals, the represented company, the equipment repaired/diagnosed, the arrival and departure times, and the assigned escort. Maintain this hard-copy of soft-copy logs for future auditing purposes.

MORE COMPLETE ANSWER: Procedural enhancements could include confirmed background checks of third-party maintainers and picture identification compared with the on-site individual. These additional enhancements should be based upon the sensitivity of the company's data. Any unattended CUI/FCI data should always be secured by CUI/FCI procedures—in a lockable container.

MP.2.119

3.8.1 Protect (i.e., physically control and securely store) information system media containing CUI, both paper and digital.

MINIMUM ANSWER: To implement this control, the business should establish procedures regarding CUI/FCI physical (paper) and virtual (disk drives) media. This should include only authorized personnel having access to individual and corporate sensitive data with necessary background checks and training. A business can use the foundations of other control families to mitigate further or reduce risks/threats.

A company can use other controls such as *more* training, longer audit log retention, *more* guards, or *more* complex passwords to **mitigate** any control. This would more clearly demonstrate to DOD that the firm has an actual implementation of these security controls.

The use of other mitigating controls within CMMC is specifically about **risk reduction.** Any effort to use other families of controls to meet a specific control improves the overall IT infrastructure's security posture and is highly recommended.

MORE COMPLETE ANSWER: Media protection controls can be further demonstrated by safeguarding physical files in secure or fire-resistant vaults. This could also include requirements for only IT personnel issuing property hand receipts for computer equipment or devices; a sound accountability system is essential.

MP.2.120

3.8.2 Limit access to CUI on information system media to authorized users.

MINIMUM ANSWER: Identify in policy documents which, by name, title, or function, has access to specified CUI//FDI. Any artifacts should include the policy document and an associated by-name roster of personnel assigned access by-system, e.g., accounting system, ordering system, patent repository, medical records, etc.

MORE COMPLETE ANSWER: A complete response could include logging authorized personnel and providing a print-out of accesses over one month.

MP.2.121
3.8.7 Control the use of removable media on information system components.

MINIMUM ANSWER: Identify in corporate policy the types and kinds of removable media attached to fixed desktop and laptop computers. These could include external hard drives, optical drives, or USB thumb drives.

Strongly recommend that thumb drives are not used; if needed, designate IT security personnel who can authorize their restricted use. This should also include anti-virus/malware scans before their use.

MORE COMPLETE ANSWER: Removeable media drives can be "blocked" by changes in system **registry** settings; company IT personnel should be able to prevent such designated devices from accessing the computer and accessing the company network.

PS.2.127
3.9.1 Screen individuals before authorizing access to information systems containing CUI.

MINIMUM ANSWER: This control requires some form of background check to be conducted for employees. Several firms can provide criminal and civil background checks based on their personal information and fingerprints.

The company should capture its HR process regarding background checks in the company cybersecurity procedure document. It is also essential to address when a reinvestigation is required. The suggestion is at least every three years or upon recognition by managers of potential legal occurrences that may include financial problems, domestic violence, etc. This control should be highly integrated with the company's HR and legal policies.

MORE COMPLETE ANSWER: Some background companies can, for an additional fee, conduct active monitoring of individuals when significant personal or financial changes occur in a person's life — update company procedural guides with all details of the company's established process.

PS.2.128

3.9.2 Ensure that CUI and information systems containing CUI are protected during and after personnel actions such as terminations and transfers.

MINIMUM ANSWER: This control is about procedures regarding whether termination is amicable or not. Always have clear terms about non-removal of corporate data and CUI/FCI after departure from the company to include databases, customer listings, and proprietary data/IP. This should consist of legal implications for violation of the policy.

MORE COMPLETE ANSWER: The technical solution could include monitoring by IT staff of all account activity during the out-processing period. This could also include immediate account lock-outs on the departure date. Also recommend that there are changes to all vault combinations, building accesses, etc., that the individual had specific access to during their tenure.

PE.2.135

3.10.2 Protect and monitor the physical facility and support infrastructure for those information systems.

MINIMUM/MORE COMPLETE ANSWER: This control can be addressed in many ways by physical security measures. This should include locked doors, cipher locks, safes, security cameras, guard forces, etc. This control should be answered by the current physical protections that prevent direct entry into the company and physical access to its IT devices and networks.

RE.2.137
(CSF PR.IP-4)

RE.2.137: Regularly perform and test data back-ups.

MINIMUM ANSWER: Depending on the system protection level (high through low), as designated by the applicable contract, full and incremental backups should happen to occur daily (high) to weekly (low) system protection levels. This should, at the latest, be a manual process being conducted by SAs or other

IT staff personnel. Data integrity testing should happen weekly to ensure that backup procedures are effectively and completely storing all data elements.

MORE COMPLETE ANSWER: A more complete solution should leverage automated backup procedures with monthly human data integrity checks.

RE.2.138

3.8.9 Protect the confidentiality of backup CUI at storage locations.
MINIMUM ANSWER: **This is a Data at Rest (DAR) issue.** See Control 3.1.3 for a depiction. See Control 3.8.6 for suggested requirements for the protection of CUI/FCI under a DAR solution.

MORE COMPLETE ANSWER: See Control 3.8.6 for additional means to protect CUI/FCI.

RM.2.141

3.11.1 Periodically assess the risk to organizational operations (including mission, functions, image, or reputation), organizational assets, and individuals resulting from the operation of organizational information systems and the associated processing, storage, or transmission of CUI.

RISK MANAGEMENT'S FOUNDATION: MITIGATE OR REDUCE, NOT ELIMINATION OF THE RISK OR THREAT

MINIMUM ANSWER: RA's are required when there is a "major" change due to either a hardware change (e.g., replacing an old firewall with a new Cisco ® firewall), software version upgrades (e.g., moving from Adobe ® 8.0 to 9.0), or changes to architecture (e.g., adding a new backup drive). The consideration is always about *how* this change to the baseline configuration is either positive (normal) or negative (preferably improbable)?

It is crucial to describe the corporate RA process regarding change needed and overall risk to the IT system. This should include who conducts the RA's technical portion and who, in senior management, for example, the Chief Operating Officer (COO) or Chief Information Officer (CIO) that determines final approval.

EXAMPLE PROCEDURE: "The RA control and actions as outlined in Annex P. The Company completed a preliminary RA (physical and virtual) occurred in 20XX—See Annex X. A subsequent RA will occur during the developmental phase of the ABC IT System in 20XX. Company RA review procedures will occur annually as of the formal declaration of a final Authority to Operate (ATO)."

This is as new to DOD Contracting as it is to the company; understand there will be "growing pains," as DOD continues to define its procedures.

While not thoroughly discussed as part of this book, **the integration of the CMMC with DOD contracting is in its infancy**. It is best to coordinate and advise DOD Contract Officers of the changes. It is always "best practice" to maintain a history of RA development and approval for future DOD auditing.

MORE COMPLETE ANSWER: Implementing a more defined RA process could include standardized formats for RA artifacts. This could consist of a technical report written by knowledgeable IT personnel about a change or a simplified form that allows for a checklist-like approach. It could also employ an outside third-party company that would formalize a review of the changes and analyzes system security's overall impact.

Changes to the Infrastructure

The Risk Assessment (RA) controls rely upon a continual process to determine whether hardware, software, or architecture changes create either a significant positive or negative **security-relevant** effect. This is typically done by using a **Change Request** (CR). Suppose an upgrade to, for example, the Windows 10 ® Secure Host Baseline Operating System software, and it improves the security posture of the network. In that case, a Risk Assessment (RA) is needed, and associated **risk analysis** should be performed by authorized technical personnel. This could take the form of a technical report that management accepts from its IT staff for approval or disapproval of the change. Management, working with its IT staff, should determine thresholds when a formal RA activity needs to occur.

The RA process affords a significant amount of flexibility during the system's life and should be used when other-than, for example, a new application or **security patches** are applied. Security patches updates are typically integrated into Operating Systems and applications. IT personnel should also regularly manually check for typical functional patches and security patch updates from the software companies' websites.

"Negative" security-relevant effects on the corporate IT infrastructure include, for example, a major re-architecture event or a move to a Cloud Service Provider. While these events may not seem "negative," NIST and DOD standards require a full reassessment. In other words, plan accordingly if the company is going to embark on a significant overhaul of its IT system. There will be a need under these circumstances to consider the impacts on the company's current ATO. These types of events typically necessitate that the CMMC process is redone; prior work in terms of policies and procedures can be reused to receive an updated ATO.

The decision-tree below is designed to help a company determine when to conduct an RA or begin an entirely new ATO/CMMC certification process:

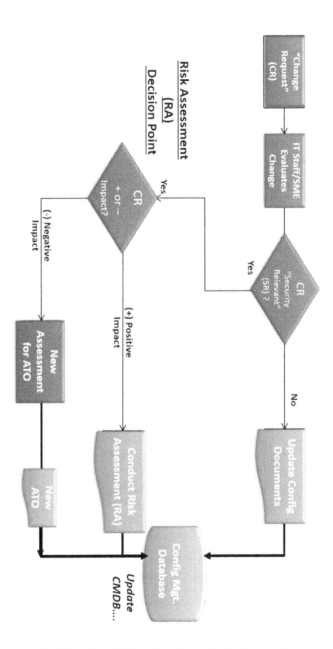

Decision-tree Addressing "Security Relevance"

RM.2.142

3.11.2 Scan for vulnerabilities in the information system and applications periodically and when new vulnerabilities affecting the system are identified.

MINIMUM ANSWER: This control requires that the company (system owner) regularly scans vulnerabilities in the information system and hosted applications based upon a defined frequency or randomly based upon an established policy or procedure. This is also supposed to be applied when new vulnerabilities affecting the system or applications are identified.

The simplest way to address this control is by using **anti-virus** and **anti-malware** enterprise-levels of software versions. Major players in these areas include Symantec ®, McAfee ®, and Malwarebytes ®. Procedural documents should describe the products used to address "new vulnerabilities" using these solutions.

MORE COMPLETE ANSWER: A suggested complete implementation could be leveraging company ISP services and providing a secondary layer of defense as a form of "trusted" connection. This could include any available SLAs that define the service provider's ability to mitigate such additional threats by employing **whitelisting** and **blacklisting** services; these services are designed to restrict access depending on an **Access Control List** (ACL). See Control 3.14.2 for a more detailed description.

RM.2.143

3.11.3 Remediate vulnerabilities in accordance with assessments of risk.

> *Cybersecurity is a leadership, not a technical challenge*

MINIMUM ANSWER: Typically, anti-virus and anti-malware security applications cannot only detect but remove and quarantine malicious software. Update documentation accordingly.

This control also addresses "vulnerabilities" created by not meeting a specific control within the CMMC. To manage these re-assessment activities, it is reasonable to update system POAM documentation with exact reasons any control is not met in full. This should attempt to answer what mitigation solutions are employed? When, by a specific date, will the vulnerability be corrected?

MORE COMPLETE ANSWER: Some additional means to better address this RA control is through other external services that can support ongoing remediation efforts. This could include the company's ISP or Cloud Service Providers. This could also include regular reviews of POAMs by management and IT support staff personnel, for example, monthly or quarterly. (See Appendix D: *Managing the Lifecycle of a POAM*).

CA.2.157

3.12.4 Develop, document, and periodically update system security plans that describe system boundaries, system environments of operation, how security requirements are implemented, and the relationships with or connections to other systems.

MINIMUM ANSWER: this control requires that the **SSP** is updated regularly. The SSP should, at a minimum, be reviewed *annually* by designated company cybersecurity/IT personnel to ensure its accuracy. The SSP should be accurately updated sooner if there are significant changes to the:

- Hardware
- Software
- Network Architecture/Topology

MORE COMPLETE ANSWER: A more complete means to address this control is by addressing company change control boards. These are regular meetings when changes to hardware, software, or architecture occur. This should include mechanisms to document the occurrence of application and security patching. An effective procedure should always address changes to the IT system.

CA.2.158

3.12.1 Periodically assess the security controls in organizational information systems to determine if the controls are effective in their application.

MINIMUM ANSWER: As described in the opening paragraph, meeting the basic requirements of the Security Assessment control should include creating a ConMon Plan and a review of 33% of the controls at least annually. (See

Appendix C for further discussion).
MORE COMPLETE ANSWER: A more thorough execution could include more than 33% of the controls being reviewed and reassessed; it is suggested to provide the results of annual Security Assessments to DOD contracting or their designated recipients.

CA.2.159

3.12.2 Develop and implement plans of action designed to correct deficiencies and reduce or eliminate vulnerabilities in organizational information systems.

MINIMUM ANSWER: Where the company does not fully implement the security control or is not recognized by DOD as fully compliant, a detailed POAM is necessary; review guidance under the AC control for a more detailed discussion of what is required in preparing a POAM for review.

As described earlier, this should include activities that are meant to answer the control in full or at least leverage other physical and virtual elements of additional security controls to reinforce the control posture in question. A well-written POAM that is tracked and managed serves as the foundation for a robust risk management process.

MORE COMPLETE ANSWER: Regular reviews by management and IT staff should enhance the company's cybersecurity posture. Cybersecurity is not just something that IT security personnel do; it includes the active oversight and review by corporate leadership to ensure effectiveness.

SC.2.178

3.13.12 Prohibit remote activation of collaborative computing devices and provide indication of devices in use to users present at the device.

MINIMUM ANSWER: Collaborative computing devices include, for example, "networked whiteboards, cameras, and microphones." The intent is to prevent these devices from being used by intruders to conduct reconnaissance of a network.

This can be prevented by changes in registry settings that only authorized IT personnel with privileged access can change. Furthermore, if these items are active, visible lighting or audible alerts should be considered to notify IT and security personnel. The policy should require that individuals do not change these settings to include privileged users. Any change should only be approved by exception and require a privileged user who is authorized to make such changes.

MORE COMPLETE ANSWER: Auditing and SIEM solutions could be configured to ensure these settings are not tampered. See Control 3.3.2 for further discussion of this topic area.

SC.2.179
(CIS specific control v7 11.5)

SC.2.79: Use encrypted sessions for the management of network devices

MINIMUM/ MORE COMPLETE ANSWER: Internal connections/sessions between servers, data stores, etc., should be encrypted even if internal to the security boundary. One recommended computer-network authentication protocol is Kerberos. This uses symmetric key cryptography and requires IT professionals with the requisite expertise to implement this as a solution.

Optional and Related NIST 800-171 Control:

3.5.10 Store and transmit only encrypted representation of passwords.
MINIMUM ANSWER: This is both a DIT and DAR issue. IT personnel should be regularly verifying that password data stores are always encrypted. This control requires that all passwords are encrypted and approved by NIST's sanctioned process under FIPS 140-2. See Control 3.13.11 for the NIST website to confirm whether a cryptographic solution is approved.

MORE COMPLETE ANSWER: Suggested greater protections could require encrypted passwords that are not collocated on the same main application or database server that stores significant portions of the business's data repository. A separate server (physical or virtual) could prevent hackers from exploits from accessing company data stores.

SI.2.214

3.14.3 Monitor information system security alerts and advisories and take appropriate actions in response.

MINIMUM ANSWER: This control can be best met through auditing. This can be achieved by using applications (such as anti-virus) or tools embedded within the architecture. These should include Intrusion Detection capabilities, network packet capture tools such as Wireshark ®, or audit logs. The process and associated actions should consist of recognition and notification to senior management. Management should ensure developed methods define when an event is raised to a level of a notifiable incident to DOD.

MORE COMPLETE ANSWER: A more-complete solution could use other advanced toolsets based on the IT support staff's education and experience. These could include malicious code protection software (such as found in more advanced anti-malware solutions). Consideration should always include the overall ROI for the investment in such tools.

Suppose the company can only implement minor portions of the control and intend to invest in improved tools in the future. In that case, it is best to develop a well-defined POAM with achievable milestones for the company to pursue. It will demonstrate to DOD a commitment to improving cybersecurity vice ignoring other technical methods to reduce the company's risk and its associated CUI/FCI.

SI.2.216

3.14.6 Monitor the information system including inbound and outbound communications traffic, to detect attacks and indicators of potential attacks.

MINIMUM ANSWER: As discussed, anti-virus and malware provide some level of checking of inbound and outbound traffic. Document both manual and automated means to ensure traffic is monitored.

Procedures should identify the people who will conduct the regular review. This process ensures proper oversight to identify violations of this control and what technologies are being used to protect inbound and outbound traffic from attack. (See Control 3.6.1 for discussion about the PPT Model and its application to address security controls).

MORE COMPLETE ANSWER: This could also identify commercial ISP's supporting the business with "trusted" connections to the Internet. Refer to provided SLA's and provided contact information for the DOD review.

SI.2.217

3.14.7 Identify unauthorized use of the information system.

MINIMUM ANSWER: This is met through active and regular auditing of, for example, systems, applications, intrusion detections, and firewall logs. It is essential to recognize that there may be limitations for the IT staff to properly and adequately review all available logs created by the company's IT network. It is best to identify the critical logs to check regularly and any secondary logs as time permits. Avoid trying to review all available system logs; there are many. Also, determine the level of effort required processing time, ability, and training of the company's IT support staff.

MORE COMPLETE ANSWER: In addition to the above, consider third-party companies that can monitor the network. While these may be expensive, they will depend on the business, its mission, and the data's critical data. This solution will require well-developed SLAs with appropriate oversight to ensure the company receives the Quality of Service (QOS) the company needs.

LEVEL 3: GOOD CYBER HYGIENE

CMMC Certification Controls

58 Security Controls/Total = 130

AC.3.017

3.1.4 Separate the duties of individuals to reduce the risk of malevolent activity without collusion.

MINIMUM ANSWER: This should be described in the corporate cybersecurity procedural document and identify the roles and responsibilities of how oversight will be executed. When this is difficult, based on the size and limited IT personnel, a POAM is highly recommended. (See Appendix D: *Managing the Lifecycle of a POAM*).

The POAM should suggest other ways to mitigate such a **risk** and potentially look at both human and automated means to address it in the future better.

MORE COMPLETE ANSWER: Individuals should be assigned *in-writing* and their roles and responsibilities. This could also include the reporting thresholds of unauthorized activities and alerted internal threats; this would better provide a more defined solution. It could also address Human Resource (HR) challenges when such incidents occur and provide a means of action against corporate policy violators.

AC.3.018

3.1.7 Prevent non-privileged users from executing privileged functions and audit the execution of such functions.

MINIMUM ANSWER: There are many apparent similarities of the controls, and that was initially designed into the CMMC for a reason. Security controls are supposed to be reinforcing, and this control is only slightly different in its scope than others described earlier.

Control 3.1.6 is similar in reinforcing this control as well as others. The company's procedure guide can explicitly "rewrite" the original control description: "Prevent non-privileged users from executing privileged functions…." An example procedure write-up based upon the original control description is provided:

EXAMPLE PROCEDURE: *Non-privileged users are prohibited from executing any privileged functions or system audits without the authority of the company's Chief Operating Officer, Chief Information Security Officer, or their designated representative. All requests will be submitted in writing with their first-line supervisor, validating the need for such access for a limited and specified time.*

Additionally, this procedure limits higher-order (privileged) functions such as creating accounts for others, deleting database files, etc. It also requires the auditing of all privileged services. It is suggested that the assigned SA at least weekly review and report inconsistencies of non-privileged/general users attempting (and, hopefully failing) to access parts of the internal infrastructure.

MORE COMPLETE ANSWER: A more thorough representation would be to provide copies of audit logs that include who, when, and the results of an audit evaluation; these artifacts should demonstrate that the company is following its internal cybersecurity procedures.

NOTE ABOUT "FREQUENCY": Many of the controls do not define how often a business should conduct a review, reassessment, etc. The business owner is allowed to "define success" to the DOD Contract Officer or cybersecurity assessor. The critical consideration is that the business determines the frequency of reviews, in general, based upon the perceived or actual sensitivity of the data. This book will typically provide the more stringent DOD frequency standard, but nothing prevents a company from conducting less frequent reviews if it can be substantiated.

Define your success

AC.3.019

3.1.11. Terminate (automatically) a user session after a defined condition.

MINIMUM ANSWER: The simplest solution is setting the SA or other designated IT personnel sets within the network's operating and management applications. Typically, most network operating systems can be set to enforce a terminal/complete lockout. This control implementation completely logs out the user and terminates any communications sessions to include, for example, access to corporate databases, financial systems, or the Internet. It requires employees to re-initiate session connections to the network after this more-complete session logout occurs.

MORE COMPLETE ANSWER: The complete answer could include screen captures of policy settings for session terminations and time-outs. The SA or designated company representative should be able to provide as an artifact.

AC.3.012

3.1.17 Protect wireless access using authentication and encryption.
MINIMUM ANSWER: Ensure this is included in the corporate procedure or policy that only authorized personnel within the firm to have access and that the appropriate encryption level is in place. Currently, the 802.11 standards are used, and Wi-Fi Protected Access 2 (WPA2) encryption should be the minimum standard.

MORE COMPLETE ANSWER: Use of Wi-Fi "sniffing technology" while available may be prohibitively costly to smaller businesses. This technology can identify and audit unauthorized entry into the wireless portion of the network and subsequently provides access to the "physical" company network. Sniffers can be used to notify security personnel either through email or Short Message Service (SMS)-text alerts of such intrusions; if company data is susceptible, then this investment may be necessary. Also, maintain any documentation about the "sniffer" and its capabilities; provide it to DOD representatives as part of the official submission.

AC.3.020

3.1.18. Control connection of mobile devices.

MINIMUM ANSWER: Most businesses' mobile devices are their cell phones. This would also include laptops and computer "pads" with web-enabled capabilities. This would first require as a matter of policy that employees only use secure connections for their devices when not using the company's service provider— these should be verified as secure. This would also explicitly bar employees from unsecured Wi-fi **hot spots** such as fast-food restaurants, coffee shops, etc. Home Wi-fi networks are typically secure but ensure that employees know to select **WPA2** as their standard at-home secure connection protocol.

MORE COMPLETE ANSWER: A better way to demonstrate this control is by discussing with the cell phone provider the ability to prevent corporate phones from using insecure Wi-Fi networks at any time. The provider should block access if the mobile phone does not "see" or recognize a secure connection. Include any proof from service agreements of such a provision as part of the submitted BOE.

AC.3.014

3.1.13 Employ cryptographic mechanisms to protect the confidentiality of remote access sessions.

MINIMUM ANSWER: **This is a Data in Transit (DIT) issue**. Ensure the procedure requires the company's solution only uses approved cryptographic solutions. The **Advanced Encryption Standard** (AES) is considered the current standard for encryption within DOD and the federal government. Also, use the 256 kilobytes (kb) key length versions.

There are many commercial solutions in this area. Major software companies provide solutions that secure DIT and are typically at reasonable prices for small business options such as Symantec ®, McAfee ®, and Microsoft®.

MORE COMPLETE ANSWER: (See Control 3.1.3 for a more detailed representation). It is usually a capability directly afforded by the remote access application tool providers. The more critical issue within DOD is whether the application tool company ensures the application is coming from a US-based software developer.

For example, there are many overseas developers, including Russia, former Warsaw Pact countries, and China, that are of concern to DOD. The apprehension is about commercial products from these nations and their potential threat to US national security. The business should confirm that the product is coming from a current ally of the US; these would include the United Kingdom, Australia, etc. *Before purchasing, ensure you have done your homework and prove that DOD accepts the remote access software.*

AC.3.021

3.1.15 Authorize remote execution of privileged commands and remote access to security-relevant information.

MINIMUM ANSWER: NIST 800-53 is the base document for all controls of the CMMC. It describes what businesses should manage and authorize privileged access to **security-relevant** information (e.g., finance information, IP, etc.) and using remote access only for "compelling operational needs."

This would explicitly be documented in the restrictions of who and under what circumstances security-relevant information may be accessed by company personnel. The base NIST control requires the business to document the rationale for this access in the System Security Plan (SSP); the interpretation is that the corporate cybersecurity policy should be an annex or appendix to the **SSP**.

MORE COMPLETE ANSWER: The ideal artifact suggested are the logs of remote access within and external to the company. This could also be found in the firewall audit logs and the remote access software application logs for comparison; these could also be used to identify log modifications that may be an indicator of **insider threat**. (See Control 3.2.3 for further discussion of this topic area).

AC.3.022

3.1.19. Encrypt CUI on mobile devices.

MINIMUM ANSWER: The good news is that all the major carriers provide DAR encryption. Mobile phones typically can secure DAR on the phone behind a passcode, PIN, or even biometric capability such as fingerprint or facial recognition; these are acceptable by DOD standards. Check service agreements or add to the company's existing plan.

MORE COMPLETE ANSWER: Several companies provide proprietary and hardened devices for corporate users. These include the state-of-the-art encryption standards, including AES-265 and SHA-256 hashing standards where possible. Further "hardened" encrypted phone sets prevent physical exploits of lost or stolen mobile devices. *Expect these solutions to be costly.*

AM.3.036

(derived from ISO 27001)

Define procedures for the handling of CUI Data.
MINIMUM ANSWER/ MORE COMPLETE ANSWER: See the Chapter in this book called: ***CUI Classification, Marking, and Storage Guide*** for a detailed presentation on how best to address this control.

What is the Value of a Data Inventory?

The System Security Plan (SSP) contains three major architectural artifacts...is it time for a fourth?

The SSP and its three sub-components are crucial elements for assessors, Authorizing Officials, and potentially future litigation. The current three are the:

- Hardware List
- Software List
- Network Diagram (or Topology)

In the age of data protection and privacy, is it not imperative we have a Data Inventory? Do companies and agencies know where and who is protecting their vital data? Data that could include privacy information, Intellectual Property (IP), Controlled Unclassified Information, personal health records, etc., need to be known not just for cybersecurity and privacy purposes but growing State requirements to protect or be FINED laws.

New York and California are expanding such laws. Specifically, current deadlines are fast approaching California and the California Consumer Protection/Privacy Act (CCPA).

It's time we add the Data Inventory

What would have to be part of such an inventory? Here are a few suggested areas that should be added to better tracking data within a company or agency's IT environment.

- Locations of all database repositories (physical locations).
- Is a Cloud Service Provider being used?
- What are specific data security protection controls being used? (NIST, ISO 27001, etc.)
- Is there shared security protection in place?
- Is there an active Service Level Agreement (SLA)?
  - How often is it reviewed?
  - How often monitored?
- The number of current records.
- Types of information stored (IP, PII, PHI, etc.)
- Whether the data is encrypted (Data at Rest (DAR) encryption requirements).
- What product is being used for DAR encryption?
- Privileged Users with elevated privilege access (System Administrators, Data Base Administrators, etc.)
- What product(s) are being used to track unauthorized access/use? (Automated audit log reviews).
- Insider Threat protections and programs.

AU.3.045
3.3.3 Review and update audited events.

MINIMUM ANSWER: This is a similar requirement to other AU controls above to review audit logs regularly. We recommend at least weekly reviews.

MORE COMPLETE ANSWER: To more completely address this control, IT personnel could categorize the collected log types. These could include an operating system (OS) (network), application, firewall, database logs, etc.

AU.3.046
3.3.4 Alert in the event of an audit process failure.

MINIMUM ANSWER: This is an active ability developed within the company's audit technology to alert personnel of an audit failure.

This could include local alarms, flashing lights, SMS, and email alerts to key company personnel. This will require SA and IT personnel to set policy settings to be established as part of the routine checks supporting the overall audit function and control. A description of the technical implementation and immediate actions to be taken by personnel should be identified. This should include the activation of the Incident Response (IR) Plan.

MORE COMPLETE ANSWER: Additional technical solutions could include supplementary systems to be monitored. This could consist of the state of all audit-capable devices and functions. This may also have a separate computer or a backup auditing server to store logs, not on the primary system; this would prevent intruders from deleting or changing logs to hide their presence in the network.

These solutions will ultimately add additional complexity and cost. Ensure any solution is supportable both financially and technically by company decision-makers. While to have greater security is an overall desire for CMMC implementation, it should be balanced with a practical and measurable value-added approach to adding any new technologies. It should also be a further consideration that incorporating new technologies should address the impacts of added complexity and determine the ability of IT support personnel to maintain it.

AU.3.048

AU.3.048: Collect audit logs into a central repository.

MINIMUM ANSWER: Store all designated logs in a central and secure repository. Also, identify the types of audit logs to be maintained. At a minimum, collect and maintain system access, anti-virus, and anti-malware logs for future attack reconstruction purposes.

MORE COMPLETE ANSWER: Use a SIEM solution to both monitor and store critical audit logs. Include log specifics as part of any log repository to include near-real-time and real-time alerts based upon the technology used to monitor network and data activities.

AU.3.049

3.3.8 Protect audit information and audit tools from unauthorized access, modification, and deletion.

MINIMUM ANSWER: This control requires greater protection of audit files and auditing tools from unauthorized users. Intruders can exploit these tools to change log files or delete them entirely to hide their entry into the system. Password protect and limit use to only authorized personnel. Document this process accordingly.

MORE COMPLETE ANSWER: This information could be stored in some other server, not part of the normal audit log capture area. Additionally, conduct regular backups to prevent intruders from manipulating logs; this will allow a means to compare changes and identify potential incidents in the network for action by senior management or law enforcement.

AU.3.050

3.3.9 Limit management of audit functionality to a subset of privileged users.

MINIMUM ANSWER: See Control 3.3.8 for reducing the numbers of personnel with access to audit logs and functions. Maintaining a roster of staff with appropriate user agreements can afford the ability to limit personnel and provide value in any future forensic activities required.

MORE COMPLETE ANSWER: Several products such as CyberArk ® could be used to manage and monitor privileged user access to audit information. This product will be a relatively expensive solution for small and some medium-sized businesses.

AU.3.051

3.3.5 Correlate audit review, analysis, and reporting processes for investigation and response to indications of inappropriate, suspicious, or unusual activity.

MINIMUM ANSWER: This should identify the technical actions taken by authorized audit personnel to pursue when analyzing suspicious activity on the network.

It should also be tied to the IR Plan and be tested at least annually. (See Control IR for further discussion of **DOD Precedence Identification** and determine actions based on the level of severity).

MORE COMPLETE ANSWER: See Control 3.3.2 for a more detailed discussion of employing a SIEM solution. In addition to manual analysis, the company could leverage the capabilities of newer threat identification technologies such as SIEM and "smart" Intrusion Detection and Prevention devices.

EXAMPLE PROCEDURE: "The Network Administrator (NWA) will notify the Information System Security Officer upon an event within 12 hours of recognition. (See DOD Precedence Categorization table). The NWA and ISSO will conduct an initial review of the log findings and determine whether it is a *categorized event*. The ISSO will notify the Program Manager within 12 hours of recognition IAW the INFINITI Incident Response Plan (IRP)—Annex F."

A standardized template may be found at
https://cybersentinel.tech/product/template-incident-response-plan-irp/

TEMPLATE:
Incident Response Plan (IRP)

AU.3.052

3.3.6 Provide audit reduction and report generation to support on-demand analysis and reporting.

MINIMUM ANSWER: Audit reduction provides for "on-demand" audit review, analysis, and reporting requirements.

This should use manual methods to collect audits from across multiple audit logging devices to assist with potential forensic needs. Any procedural effort to support audit reduction most likely can use commercial support applications and scripts (small programs typically are explicitly written to the business's unique IT environment) that IT personnel should assist in their identification, development, and procurement.

MORE COMPLETE ANSWER: IT personnel could identify more automated and integrated audit reduction solutions. Likely candidates could be "smart" firewalls or Security Information and Event Management (SIEM) solutions.

AT.3.058

3.2.3 Provide security awareness training on recognizing and reporting potential indicators of insider threat.

MINIMUM ANSWER: The DOD's Defense Security Service (DSS) in Quantico, VA, is the executive agent for insider threat activities. The DSS provides many training opportunities and toolkits on Insider Threats. These are available from their agency website for free at http://www.dss.mil/it/index.html. This is an excellent resource for creating an insider threat training program already developed for its use.

(DSS was re-designated as the Defense Counterintelligence and Security Agency [DCSA] October 1, 2019. https://www.dcsa.mil/).

Document company minimum training requirements for general and privileged users, such as watching select online instruction or computer-based training opportunities from DSS. Everyone in the company should participate and satisfactorily complete the training.

MORE COMPLETE ANSWER: More-complete proof of company compliance with this security control requirement might include guest speakers or insider threat brown-bag events around lunchtime. Company training personnel should capture attendance records to have sign-in rosters. These could be used for annual training requirements specific to insider threat familiarity.

Also, recommend a **train-the-trainer program** where select individuals are trained by either DSS or other competent company that becomes corporate resources. These assigned individuals could provide training and first-responder support as needed and be deployed to other company sites.

CM.3.067

3.4.5 Define, document, approve, and enforce physical and logical access restrictions associated with changes to the information system.
MINIMUM/MORE COMPLETE ANSWER: "Access restrictions" are aligned with the earlier discussed AC controls. As part of a corporate CM policy, any IT baseline changes need to be captured within a formal process approved by that process and documented. Documentation is typically maintained in a CM database, and more specifically, it would require the update of any hardware or software lists. Proof of compliance would be the production of updated listings that are maintained by the CM database. This should include updating any network diagrams describing in a graphic form a description of the corporate network; these are all explicit requirements under CMMC. These artifacts should also be included in the **SSP**.

CM.3.068

3.4.7 Restrict, disable, and prevent the use of nonessential programs, functions, ports, protocols, and services.
MINIMUM ANSWER: Nonessential programs, functions, ports, and protocols are prime attack avenues for would-be hackers. Any programs that are not used for the conduct of business operations should be removed. Where that is not possible, these programs should be blacklisted to run in the company's IT environment. (See 3.4.8. below).

Regarding ports and protocols, this will require IT staff direct involvement in the decision-making process. Specific ports are typically needed for any 21st Century company's daily operation. For example, ports 80, 8080, and 443 are used to send HTTP (web traffic); these ports will typically be required to be active.

Port Number	Application Supported
20	File Transport Protocol (FTP) Data
23	Telnet
25	Simple Mail Transfer Protocol (SMTP)
80, 8080, 443	Hypertext Transport Protocol (HTTP) → WWW
110	Post Office Protocol version 3 (POP3)

Common Ports and Their Associated Protocols

Those ports and protocols that are not required should be closed by designated IT personnel. This prevents hackers from exploiting open entries into the corporate infrastructure. Ensure a copy of all open and closed ports is readily available to DOD representatives for review as part of CMMC requirements.

MORE COMPLETE ANSWER: The business could employ tools that check for unused and open ports. This could include a regular reassessment of whether ports need to remain active. As mentioned earlier, products such as Wireshark ® could be used as a low-cost solution to conduct any reassessment of the corporate infrastructure.

EXAMPLE PROCEDURE: "Only Ports, Protocols, and Services (PPS) required for INFINITI operations are activated by the assigned BH System/Network Administrator. All non-required PPSs will be deactivated. All nonessential software programs and functionality installed is controlled by an application whitelisting solution.

There are currently 4 (four) active operational; all others are closed. <u>Currently, only ports 8080 (http), 443 (https), 123 (ntp), and 53 (dns) are active.</u>"

The 5 Most Attacked Ports Survey

Virtual ports within a computer architecture are intended to provide software applications the ability to share memory and data resources effectively (Mitchell, 2019). These ports range in the thousands and are designed to prevent interference with other computer activities of the multitude of applications run by the user. They are of concern, especially about networking with the Internet, where they are exposed to external threats and activities. The survey down-selected the top 5 ports universally hacked (Beaver, 2016; Security Trails, 2019; Weiss, 2017; XeusHack, 2017). Based upon several Internet-based sources, the following five crucial ports were selected:

COLUMN:	A	B	C	D	E
Reference:	(Beaver, 2016)	(Security Trails, 2019)	(Weiss, 2017)	(Xeus Hack, 2017)	2020 Rankings
File Transfer Protocol (FTP) – Port 21	1	1	1	1	1
Secure Shell (SSH) – Port 22	2	2	2	2	2
Telnet – Port 23	3	3	3	3	3
Simple Mail Transfer Protocol (SMTP) – Port 25	4	4	4	4	4
Domain Name System (DNS) – Port 53	5	5	5	5	5

References:

Beaver, K. (2016, March 26). Commonly hacked ports[Blog post]. *Dummies*. Retrieved from https://www.dummies.com/programming/networking/commonly-hacked-ports/

Security Trails. (2019, May 7). Top 20 and 200 most scanned ports in the cybersecurity industry [Blog post]. *Security Trails*. Retrieved from https://securitytrails.com/blog/top-scanned-ports

Weiss, J. (2017, March 7). Vulnerability by common ports dashboard [Blog post]. *Tenable*. Retrieved from https://www.tenable.com/blog/vulnerabilities-by-common-ports-dashboard

Xeushack. (2017, January 20). The ultimate hacking cheat sheet: Work smarter, not harder [Blog post]. *Xeushack*. Retrieved from http://xeushack.com/the-ultimate-hacking-cheat-sheet

CM.3.069

3.4.8 Apply deny-by-exception (blacklist) policy to prevent the use of unauthorized software or deny all, permit-by-exception (whitelisting) policy to allow the execution of authorized software.

MINIMUM/MORE COMPLETE ANSWER: The company should employ **blacklisting** or **whitelisting** (See Control 3.14.2 for more information) to prohibit the execution of unauthorized software programs or applications within the information system. A copy of the current listing should be part of the formal Body of Evidence (BOE).

IA.3.083

3.5.3 Use multifactor authentication for local and network access to privileged accounts and for network access to non-privileged accounts.

MINIMUM ANSWER: See Control 3.5.2 above. Ensure the requirement for MFA or 2FA is part of the company's cybersecurity policy/procedure.

MORE COMPLETE ANSWER: (See Control 3.5.2 for suggested approaches).

IA.3.084

3.5.4 Employ replay-resistant authentication mechanisms for network access to privileged and nonprivileged accounts.

MINIMUM ANSWER: This control requires replay-resistant technologies to prevent replay attacks. **Replay attacks** are also known as a **playback attacks**. This is an attack where the hacker captures legitimate traffic from an authorized user, presumably a positively identified network user, and uses it to gain unauthorized access to a network. This is also considered a form of a **Man-in-the-Middle** type attack.

The most natural solution to resolving this control is to have company IT personnel disable **Secure Socket Layer (SSL)**—which DOD no longer authorizes. Businesses should use the **Transport Layer Security (TLS) 1.0** or higher; as a required DOD standard.

If the business needs to continue using SSL to maintain connectivity with, for example, external or third-party data providers, a POAM is required. Efforts should be made to discuss with these data providers when they will no longer be using SSL. This discussion should begin as soon as possible to advise DOD through a POAM that demonstrates the company is conducting its proper due diligence to protect its CUI/FCI.

MORE COMPLETE ANSWER: A potentially expensive solution could include the addition of a **SIEM** solution. Many major IT network providers have added artificial intelligence capabilities to detect this type of attack better; identify any solution carefully.

IA.3.085

3.5.5 Prevent reuse of identifiers for a defined period.

MINIMUM ANSWER: This IA control directs that "individual, group, role, or device identifiers" are reused. This should be included as part of any written procedure and defined in system policies to prevent identifiers from reuse. This could consist of email address names (individual), administrator accounts (group), or device identifiers such as "finan_db" designating a high-value target such as a "financial database" (device).

This control prevents intruders who have gained information about such identifiers from having less of a capability to use this information for an exploit of the business. This will help better thwart a hacker's intelligence collection and analysis of a company's internal network. This control is designed to prevent intruders' ability to access corporate systems and their resident CUI//FCI repositories.

MORE COMPLETE ANSWER: Reuse of individual identifiers should be discouraged, for example, in the case of a returning employee. This is an essential suggestion: 'John.Smith@cui-company.com' could be varied examples, 'John.H.Smith2@cui-company.com.

IA.3.086

3.5.6 Disable identifiers after a defined period of inactivity.

MINIMUM/MORE COMPLETE ANSWER: This requires that the system terminates its connection after a defined time-out setting. The recommendation is 30 minutes maximum, but as mentioned earlier, the time-out should always be based on data sensitivity.

IA.3.098

3.6.2 Track, document, and report incidents to appropriate officials and/or authorities both internal and external to the organization.

MINIMUM ANSWER: This control discusses the reporting requirements based on the severity of the incident described above and within DOD's Precedence Categorization above. Ensure some form of the repository is maintained that an auditor could review at any time. Another reminder is that such information should be secured and encrypted, at least at the CUI/FCI level.

MORE COMPLETE ANSWER: A complete response may include a dedicated computer server repository that could be physically disconnected from the system when not needed. This could prevent unauthorized access if an intruder attempts to conduct intelligence collection or **reconnaissance** of the system; this would deny intruders' critical network information and add confusion for their penetration activities.

IA.3.099

3.6.3 Test the organizational incident response capability.

MINIMUM ANSWER: Test the IR Plan at least **annually**. This should include both internal and external notional penetration exercises. These may consist of compromised login information and passwords provided to designated IT personnel. Ensure the results of the test are documented, reviewed, and signed by senior management. An IR test event should be maintained for any future audit.

MORE COMPLETE ANSWER: This is not a requirement of this control and poses many risks to the IT environment. Do not recommend this solution; this would only be required based on data sensitivity, and the DOD directs penetration Testing (PENTEST). It is only offered for more of an appreciation of the complexity that a PENTEST entails.

A more expensive solution is hiring an outside Penetration Testing (PENTEST) company. Ensure that Rules of Engagement (ROE) are well established. Rules that should be affirmed by both the company and the PENTESTER, for example, is that no inadvertent change or destruction of data is authorized. The PENTEST company may also require a liability release for any unintentional damage caused by the PENTEST. Always coordinate with legal professionals experienced in such matters to avoid any damage or confusion created by a PENTEST's unclear expectations.

MA.3.115

3.7.3 Ensure equipment removed for off-site maintenance is sanitized of any CUI.

MINIMUM ANSWER: Company data should be backed-up locally and secured for a future reinstall on another storage device or the returned/repaired IT component. Also, the data should specifically be "wiped" by an industry-standard application for data deletion. Many software tools conduct multiple "passes" of data wipes to ensure the sanitization of the media.

MORE COMPLETE ANSWER: Any reports produced by the data "wiping" program could be captured in an equipment data log to prove the action. Maintaining a hard copy of a soft copy spreadsheet or database log would be helpful. Future inspections by DOD may check this procedure to confirm the continuous application and repeatability of this procedure.

MA.3.116

3.7.4 Check media containing diagnostic and test programs for malicious code before the media are used in the information system.

MINIMUM ANSWER: The ideal solution for this is to conduct a scan using corporate anti-virus software applications.

MORE COMPLETE ANSWER: A more comprehensive solution would include the use of an anti-malware application. Anti-malware programs are more extensive and proactively monitor **endpoints**, i.e., computers, laptops, servers, etc. (Anti-virus is not always designed to identify and clean malware, adware, worms, etc., from infected storage devices).

MP.3.122

3.8.4 Mark media with necessary CUI markings and distribution limitations.

MINIMUM ANSWER: This includes the marking of both physical documents as well as soft-copy versions. The best way to answer this is by referencing the following National Archives and Record Administration (NARA) document as part of the company's procedural guide that addresses this control:

- *See Chapter on CUI Marking and Handling.*
- *Marking Controlled Unclassified Information*, Version 1.1 – December 6, 2016. (https://www.archives.gov/files/cui/20161206-cui-marking-handbook-v1-1.pdf)

***EXAMPLE PROCEDURE:** All company personnel will mark CUI/FCI, physical and virtual data, per the National Archives and Record Administration (NARA), <u>Marking Controlled Unclassified Information, Version 1.1 – December 6, 2016</u>. If there are questions about marking requirements, employees will refer these questions to their immediate supervisor or the corporate CUI/FCI officer.*

MORE COMPLETE ANSWER: This could include a screen capture that shows a DOD representative that onscreen access to CUI/FCI data is appropriately marked. A firm could also assign a CUI/FCI marking specialist; this person should be an individual with prior security experience and familiar with DOD marking requirements. For example, this individual could additionally provide quarterly "brown bag" sessions where the "CUI/FCI Security Officer" provides training during lunchtime sessions. Be creative when considering more thorough means to reinforce cybersecurity control requirements.

MP.3.123

3.8.8 Prohibit the use of portable storage devices when such devices have no identifiable owner.

MINIMUM ANSWER: This should be established in the company procedure. If such devices are found, they should be surrendered to security and scanned immediately for viruses, malware, etc.

MORE COMPLETE ANSWER: As described in Control 3.8.7, IT personnel can block unauthorized devices from attaching to the computer/network by updating registry settings.

MP.3.124

3.8.5 Control access to media containing CUI and maintain accountability for media during transport outside of controlled areas.

MINIMUM ANSWER: This control is about "transport outside of controlled areas." This, too, is a matter of only authorized individuals (couriers) be approved by position, training, and security checks that should be considered when the company needs to transport CUI/FCI external to its typical corporate location.

Individuals should be provided either courier cards or orders signed by an authorized company representative typically responsible for oversight of security matters. This could be, for example, the corporate security officer, Information System Security Manager (ISSM), or their designated representative. These individuals should be readily known to other employees and managers who have demanded to move CUI/FCI to outside locations. This would demonstrate that there are available and on-call personnel based on the business mission and priorities. This also should be a limited cadre of staff that management relies on for such external courier services.

MORE COMPLETE ANSWER: The company could hire an outside contract service that transports physical and computer media containing CUI/FCI based on its mission.

MP.3.125

3.8.6 Implement cryptographic mechanisms to protect the confidentiality of CUI stored on digital media during transport unless otherwise protected by alternative physical safeguards.

MINIMUM ANSWER: This is a Data at Rest (DAR) issue. See Control 3.1.3 for depiction. The recommendation is that all CUI/FCI needs to be encrypted. A typical application that DOD has used is BitLocker ®. It provides password protection to "lockdown" any transportable media. It is not the only solution, and many answers can be used to secure DAR.

The 256-bit key length is the common standard for commercial and DOD encryption applications for hard drives, removable drives, and even USB devices. DOD requires DAR must always be encrypted; it is best to resource and research proper tools that DOD supports and recognizes.

MORE COMPLETE ANSWER: The reinforcement of this control may include using enhanced physical security measures. This could consist of hardened and lockable carry cases. Only authorized employees should transport designated CUI/FCI. This should also be captured in the submitted BOE to DOD.

PE.3.136

3.10.6 Enforce safeguarding measures for CUI at alternate worksites (e.g., telework sites).

MINIMUM ANSWER: (See Control 3.1.3 for the explanation of DAR and DIT). DAR application solutions can quickly address this control. Laptops should always be password protected; this should be part of any central cybersecurity policy document and enforced by technical solutions deployed by company IT personnel. Additionally, The DIT protections are afforded by corporate VPN and 2FA/MFA solutions.

MORE COMPLETE ANSWER: The company should establish minimum requirements for telework protection. This could include, for example, work that should be conducted in a physically securable area. The VPN should always be used. Corporate assets should not use unsecured networks such as at coffee shops, fast-food restaurants, etc. This could also include an explicit telework agreement for employees before being authorized telework permission, and it should be carefully coordinated with HR and legal experts.

RE.3.139
(CIS Control v7.1)

RE.3.139: Regularly perform complete and comprehensive data back-ups and store them off-site and off-line.

MINIMUM ANSWER: Conduct daily backups for high sensitivity and weekly backups of low sensitivity IT programs. Ensure regular full backups are used with incremental daily backups based upon the data's sensitivity; coordinate with the

KO/CO and the project manager to identify storage requirements. Off-site backups should be at least 75 miles from the primary data servers.

MORE COMPLETE ANSWER: Execute the above guidance and ensure that data storage is at least 100 miles from the primary data server site.

RM.3.144
(CERT RMM v1.2 RISK:SG3 and SG4.SP3)

RM.3.144: Periodically perform risk assessments to identify and prioritize risks according to the defined risk categories, risk sources, and risk measurement criteria.

MINIMUM ANSWER: An overall Risk Assessment Report (RAR) should be developed for all CMMC systems. The RAR identifies significant systems, networks, and data risks. Risk should be identified in the form of a risk matrix. The number of risks identified and scored should be based upon the complexity and threats (both internal and external) to the IT system.

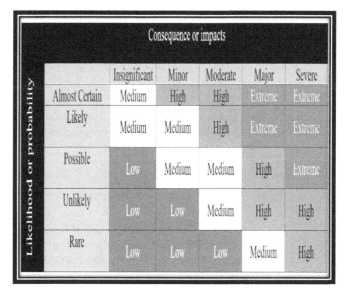

The Risk Matrix

MORE COMPLETE ANSWER: Individual Risk Assessments should be accomplished for all major system components. This should include the computer, major peripherals, and sensors of the system.

Example RAs are provided below to review secure code and system development processes that align with RMF and CMMC's expected reporting standards.

Risk Assessment (RA) Component Template

THRU: Ms. Smith, Information Systems Security Officer
FOR: Program Manager, Small-Widgets
FROM: Information Security Engineer, Bob New Hart, PE

RISK ANALYSIS FOR: The <u>Space Vehicle's Navigation and Communications subsystem</u> of the USSS 2020 System.

Executive Summary

A Risk Analysis was completed on XX February XXXX for the <u>Space Vehicle's Navigation and Communications subsystem.</u> The static code review provided multiple artifacts to include the outputs from its preliminary and final reports. The final report identified nearly 100% correction (1 open warning) of any software coding weaknesses or vulnerabilities. **Recommend approval.**

Objective

- Recommend that Assessors [AUDITORS] conduct a review of provided artifacts and approve and accept this Risk Assessment (RA) per Risk Management Framework (RMF) specific to the RA-3 control.
- Request approval from Assessors [AUDITORS] about the current effort to implement and create a formalized RA process supporting the USSS 2020 program.

Analysis

The vendor and its subcontractor completed an *excellent* "static code" review and artifacts demonstration by RMF Control SA-11. The artifacts provided should become the basis and archetype for any future like RA efforts. The quality of the work completed specific to the <u>Space Vehicle's Navigation and Communications subsystem</u> should be used to develop a more-defined RA process. The intent is to increase the security posture of the USSS 2020 in total and continue to help guide vendors to meet policy and contractual requirements.

1. RA Background Information:

    a. Risk Assessments are required throughout the system's life and are supposed to be updated as risks and threats change against the specific system. These risks include version or build changes that occur during the normal process of maintaining and enhancing the system's readiness to meet customer requirements.

    b. System changes are required to be reflected in an updated RA IAW RMF control: <u>RA-3</u>. This includes "... modifications to the information system or environment of operation (including the identification of new threats and vulnerabilities) or other conditions that may impact the security state of the system.

    c. A current process development effort is currently underway with the USSS 2020 and its subsystems. The initiative requires some level of certainty of secure software development through formal artifacts provided by the developer.

    d. The following documents are considered candidates that address security in full or part by the developer:

        i. Changes impacting TRUSTED SOFTWARE DEVELOPMENT PROCESS (TSDP) hardware/components. This should include some form of attestation (signed) artifact by senior software development/quality assurance leadership that such development is in conformance with the Government approved secure process.

ii. Completed Security Technical Implementation Guide (STIG) checklists for the APPLICATION SECURITY DEVELOPMENT (APPSECDEV) STIG for all software. It should be signed and approved by the vendor's senior software development/quality assurance leadership.

iii. Static code review of source code by government/industry-recognized tool.

iv. Outputs from the tool include an executive summary of findings and raw data subject to data rights limitations.

e. <u>Space Vehicle's Navigation and Communications subsystem</u> Software Risk Analysis:

i. The artifact/file, <u>Code-Analysis-Pre-Findings-rpt.pdf (See Attachment 1 for a listing of all artifacts)</u>, dated XX March 20XX, identified that the commercial static code analysis tool, CodeSonar2 (See Attachment 2), was used. The 8-software code sub-modules identified <u>397 active warnings</u> across 220 total files per submodule. Of concern for cybersecurity purposes are the buffer overruns and integer overflows; the findings and numbers were constant across all submodules.

ii. CodeSonar2 Analysis Report dated XX June 20XX, <u>Code-Analysis-Final-rpt.pdf</u>, identifies <u>0</u> active warnings after assuming coding updates were satisfactorily accomplished. In this report, the outputs were parsed based on files versus submodule but identified the file count of 220 in Table 1, Summary for Recent Analyses. There were 220 total files scanned.

iii. In the Final Certification Report, <u>Final-Review-report.pdf</u>, XX November XXXX, all false positives were addressed, and only one final warning regarding "uninitialized variables" was identified in the file:

oef_cobol213_string.cxx. While uninitialized variables pose a security risk, associated mitigating protections would protect the overall USSS 2020 from most outside cyber-attacks.

iv. Additionally, a Penetration Test was accomplished against the sub-system. While not required at the sub-system level, it demonstrates additional due diligence on the developer's part. The results of that effort appear acceptable.

v. Overall, it is reasonable to assume that all code functionality repairs, including high-interest security coding corrections, have been satisfactorily accomplished. Any risk to the <u>Space Vehicle's Navigation and Communications subsystem is suggested below.</u>

Conclusion

Request approval of a favorable RA for the <u>Space Vehicle's Navigation and Communications subsystem</u> of the USSS 2020 System.

EXAMPLE ONLY

RM.3.146
(CERT RMM v1.2 RISK:SG5:SP1)

RM.3.146: Develop and implement risk mitigation plans.

MINIMUM ANSWER/MORE COMPLETE ANSWERS: Risk mitigation plans should be tied to the Risk matrix described under CMMC Control C031/P1144. Plans should focus on the three major programmatic categories. Example questions are provided to help develop mitigation plans and actions.

- Performance
    - How to respond to a loss of extended loss of power or connectivity?
    - What actions are required to support alternate sites and backup procedures for lost or compromised data?
- Schedule
    - How to respond to crucial components not being available to support operations promptly? Alternate vendors?
    - How to recover from a catastrophic outage within 48 hours?
- Cost
    - How to provide engaged capabilities and remain within budget?
    - How to keep service calls to less than 25 hours per month?

RM.3.147
(CMMC-specific)

RM.3.147: Manage non-vendor supported products (e.g., end of life) separately and restrict as necessary to reduce risk.

MINIMUM ANSWER: Track all hardware and especially software nearing end-of-life (EOL). This should be part of the organization's configuration management process to track components that will no longer be under existing or future warranties.

MORE COMPLETE ANSWER: Develop policies to address components that are one-year, six-month, and 90-days from EOL. Create a manual or automated tracking tool and provide key company and federal leadership at least every 90-days.

Furthermore, develop processes to ensure that products are being purchased from reputable manufacturers and vendors. Create a Supply Chain Diligence Team (SCDT) to oversee the US and foreign IT equipment and product purchases. (See the 2019 SCRM 2.0 book at Amazon® https://www.amazon.com/SCRM-2-0-Century-Management-Solutions/dp/1093992670/ref=sr_1_1?keywords=scrm+2.0&qid=1581090210&sr=8-1.

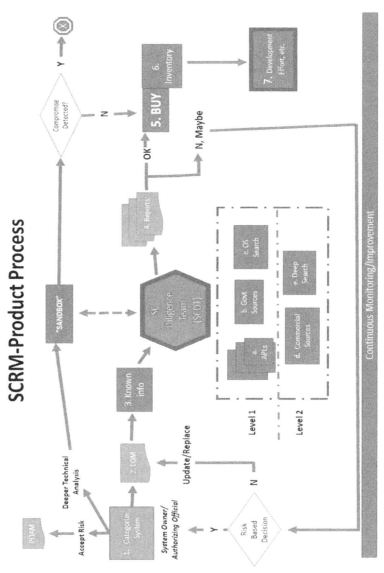

The Supply Chain Risk Management (SCRM)-Product Process is provided as an initial guide to companies and agencies (See the book, SCRM 2.0, on Amazon)

CA.3.161

3.12.3 Monitor information system security controls on an ongoing basis to ensure the continued effectiveness of the controls.

MINIMUM ANSWER: This control can be answered in terms of a well-developed and executed ConMon Plan. Describing its purpose and the actions of assigned personnel to accomplish this task will answer this control.

MORE COMPLETE ANSWER: Suggested additional efforts regarding this control could include ad hoc spot checks of controls outside of the annual review process. Identify using the **PPT Model** described in Control 3.6.1 who is responsible for conducting the assessment (people), the workflow to adequately assess the current state of the control (process), and any supporting automation that provides feedback and reporting to management (technology).

CA.3.162

CA.3.162: Employ a security assessment of enterprise software that has been developed internally, for internal use, and that has been organizationally defined as an area of risk.

MINIMUM ANSWER: The basic requirements of the Security Assessment control should include creating a ConMon Plan and a review of 33% of the controls at least annually.

For this control, CMMC directs the development of an internal policy specific to an application and executable development. This should include real-time scans of the internal IT environment looking for vulnerabilities. More specifically, a SA is used to determine the impacts of adding or removing software and its operational and security implications to the overall system's viability.

MORE COMPLETE ANSWER: This would require static and dynamic code review tools by contracted developers. Products, such as HP Fortify®, a rather pricey option, can be used by developers to find vulnerabilities such as buffer overflows and SQL injection weaknesses. There are free software tools that can also be used.

RMF is about Risk Management, not necessarily, Risk Elimination.

SA.3.169
(CMMC-specific)

SA.3.169: Receive and respond to cyber threat intelligence from information sharing forums and sources and communicate to stakeholders.

MINIMUM ANSWER: Develop processes on how to incorporate internal and external threat information for responses to cyber-threats. This should be part of a developed IRP.

MORE COMPLETE ANSWER: Consider the implementation of STIX 2.0 as part of a cyber-threat intelligence effort.

Structured Threat Information eXpression (STIX) providing External Data to Industry for Information Sharing

One U.S. government's attempt to introduce external data to both the public and private sectors is developing the STIX formatting standard in 2010 (MITRE, 2010). A significant finding of the 9-11 Commission was the lack of *information sharing* between the various members of federal law enforcement and the intelligence community in anticipating the fateful attack of September 11, 2001 (Director of National Intelligence [DNI], 2018; National Commission on Terrorist Attacks upon the United States [NCTAUS], 2004).

The US government championed the STIX effort to provide more effective communications of cyber-threat data among organizations. The initiative was launched by the Department of Homeland Security (DHS) to create STIX (MITRE, n.d.; HSSEDI, n.d.). The STIX format development met the exchange needs of threat intelligence between the federal government and the private sector. It was formulated to support cyber-threat intelligence so it "can be shared, stored, and analyzed in a consistent manner" (STIX Project, 2018). "STIX is a collaborative, community-driven effort to define and develop a structured language to represent cyber threat information" (MITRE, n.d.). It was meant to foster closer coordination between the private and public sectors regarding cybersecurity activities incorporated by ML tools and techniques to assist predictive analytics better.

However, as Waterman (2017) describes the ongoing failure of information sharing attempts by the federal government, he reports that "everyone wants to receive information, but few are prepared to make an effort to give back" (para. 1). The 2015 Cybersecurity Act offered a "safe harbor for companies" and federal protections from litigation for divulging penetrations or vulnerabilities into an organization's network (para. 5). However, most firms' desire still exists to avoid reporting for its reputational and ultimate profitability impacts to a business (Waterman, 2017).

This weakness in information sharing adds to the challenges of cybersecurity protection measures. However, as Kulp (2019) suggests, information sharing and external intelligence are vital to any threat response. Improved threat data distribution has a relationship with the long-term need and premise of this study; if time-sensitive data is not available, the threat will continue to exploit network gaps faster than the cyber-defenders. *It requires a universal allocation of time-sensitive data to be effective.*

SC.3.177

3.13.11 Employ FIPS-validated cryptography when used to protect the confidentiality of CUI.

MINIMUM/MORE COMPLETE ANSWER: The company needs to confirm that its encryption applications are FIPS 140-2 compliant[15]. It can easily be verified at

---

[15] Note: FIPS 140-2 will be retired in 2021 and be replaced by FIPS 140-3. This should not affect the FIP Validation Program data search site.

the website below:

Official NIST site to confirm FIPS 140-2 cryptographic compliance
(https://csrc.nist.gov/projects/cryptographic-module-validation-program/validated-modules/search)

SC.3.180

3.13.2 Employ architectural designs, software development techniques, and systems engineering principles that promote effective information security within organizational information systems.

MINIMUM/MORE COMPLETE ANSWER: Describing effective security architectural design measures can be as simple as establishing a properly configured firewall or 2FA/MFA utilized by the company. Especially within DOD, the accepted best practice is the principle of Defense in Depth (DID). This philosophy should be easily implemented by IT staff and understandable by organizational leadership in protecting CUI data. The average company seeking contracts with DOD will likely be specifically concerned with primary and secure architectures.

Other **mitigation** elements that can be described for this control may include physical security measures (e.g., a 24-hour guard force, reinforced fire doors, and cameras) or blacklist measures that prevent unauthorized applications from executing in the corporate network. See Control 3.13.10 for how 2FA operates internal or external to a company's system.

EXAMPLE PROCEDURE: "The Company Employs Defense in Depth (DID) as the basis of all security measures. It begins with security and awareness training of all companies directly or indirectly supporting the ABC IT System. Access control measures and associated auditing ensures Identity Management and accountability of only those personnel with the need to access the system.

Active technical measures include smart firewall solutions that protect the application, database, and services through whitelisting as one of many efforts to ensure the system's security. Cloud-based solutions such as ESET and associated AWS services provide real-time technical protection of the IT security boundary. Finally, the philosophy is also of Continuous Monitoring of the IT environment. The company uses both manual and automated capabilities of the system to protect critical data from compromise. The Company is committed to the absolute security, privacy, and protection of CUI/FCI data IAW customer requirements and direction.

Additionally, the ABC IT System also employs SNORT for Intrusion Detection/Prevention Systems (IDS/IPS)."

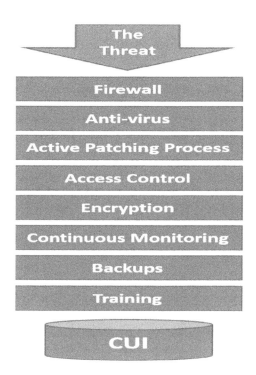

The Principle of Defense in Depth

SC.3.181

3.13.3 Separate user functionality from information system management functionality.

MINIMUM ANSWER: The policy should not allow privileged users to use the same credentials to access their users (e.g., email and Internet searches) and privileged user access. This separation of access is a basic network security principle and is intended to hamper insider and external threats. (A suggested review of a similar control in Control 3.1.4, and its discussion of the **segregation of duty** or **separation of duties** principle for comparison.)

MORE COMPLETE ANSWER: There are technical solutions to automate this process. For example, CyberArk ® is used in many parts of the federal government to track and account for privileged user activity that is easily auditable. The ability to oversee, especially privileged user activity, should be readily audited and reviewed by senior company cybersecurity representatives.

SC.3.182

3.13.4 Prevent unauthorized and unintended information transfer via shared system resources.

MINIMUM ANSWER: **Peer-to-peer** networking is not authorized within the DOD, and it is strongly suggested the corporation's network also forbids its use. This is typically part of the AUP and should be enforceable to prevent, e.g., insider threat opportunities or used by external hackers to gain unauthorized access using legitimate employee security credentials.

MORE COMPLETE ANSWER: Suggest that this is part of the regular audit activity by designated IT personnel. They could be reviewing audit logs for unauthorized connections to include peer-to-peer networking.

SC.3.183

3.13.6 Deny network communications traffic by default and allow network communications traffic by exception (i.e., deny all, permit by exception).

MINIMUM/MORE COMPLETE ANSWER: Like Control 3.4.8, this control can be selected by IT personnel. This is a technical control that should also be captured in the procedure document. These network settings are typically set at the firewall and involve **whitelisting** (only permitting access by exception) and **blacklisting**[16] (from non-authorized Internet addresses) everyone else to enter the network. (Also, review Control 3.14.2).

SC.3.184

3.13.7 Prevent remote devices from simultaneously establishing non-remote connections with the information system and communicating via some other connection to resources in external networks.

MINIMUM/MORE COMPLETE ANSWER: If a teleworking employee uses their remote device (i.e., notebook computer) and then connects to a non-remote (external) connection, it allows for an unauthorized external connection to exist;

---

[16] BLACKLISTING is highly inefficient in protecting IT environments. It becomes a growing database of blocked IP addresses. The preferred best practice is the WHITELISTING which is far more efficient in controlling and allowing only authorized external connections from approved users and sites.

this provides a potential hacker with the ability to enter the network using the authorized employee's credentials.

It is critical that the company requires employees to use their VPN connection and blocks any insecure connections from accessing internal systems or applications. IT personnel need to ensure these settings are correctly configured and are part of the corporate cybersecurity procedure documentation.

SC.3.185

3.13.8 Implement cryptographic mechanisms to prevent unauthorized disclosure of CUI during transmission unless otherwise protected by alternative physical safeguards.

MINIMUM ANSWER: Remember, this control is about external communications from the network and its system boundary. This is a DIT issue and is protected by the cryptographic solutions discussed earlier; see Control 3.1.3. Documentation should reflect the type and level of protection of data transmitted. Any additional protections such as a VPN, a secure circuit/dedicated circuit provided by a commercially contracted carrier may afford more security for company data transmissions.

MORE COMPLETE ANSWER: Better protection levels could be addressed regarding defense-in-depth, which is a current operational philosophy supported by DOD; additional layers of security provide extra defense.

SC.3.186

3.13.9 Terminate network connections associated with communications sessions at the end of the sessions or after a defined period of inactivity.

MINIMUM ANSWER: This was addressed in the AC control specific to the complete termination of a session. Sessions of suggested importance would be those such as the financial, HR, or other essential computer server systems housing defined CUI/FCI. It is recommended that the procedure is explicitly updated to this control, re-using language provided by any response to the control(s) discussing the termination of a network connection.

MORE COMPLETE ANSWER: Audit of sessions that have timed-out can strengthen this control. SA's and IT staff can determine from audit logs that the prescribed time-out period was met and enforced. Provide a sampling to any DOD inspector as part of the final packet.

SC.3.187

3.13.10 Establish and manage cryptographic keys for cryptography employed in the information system.

MINIMUM ANSWER: There are two significant scenarios likely to occur:

1. The use of commercial cryptographic programs that resides within the company's architecture or is provided by an external "managed service" provider is the most likely scenario. The keys will be maintained and secured by the cryptographic application. The company is establishing some form of 2FA solution. The public key would be obtained somewhere else in the architecture, and the private key that of the employee would reside on a token such as a CAC card or another critical device.

2. Using a DOD or other like 2FA solution with a CAC, Personal Identity Verification (PIV) card, or "token" such as those produced by RSA ® is likely if DOD authorizes the exchange of keys on its systems with that of the company. This requires a Certificate Authority (CA) usually outside the local network either managed by DOD or another trusted commercial entity with the capability to support "asymmetric" 2FA.

Whichever solution is used, ensure compatibility with DOD systems and other companies as part of its normal operations. ***All transmittal of CUI/FCI data is required to be encrypted.***

MORE COMPLETE ANSWER: Any more exceptional ability to secure and protect the **company's key store** or through defined SLA's with outside service providers is essential. Ensure they have safeguards in place to protect unauthorized access to its system. They may use more robust encryption methods, but ensure they are recognized by DOD and are Federal Information Processing Standards (FIPS 140-2) compliant. (See Control 3.13.11 for identifying FIPS 140-2 solutions).

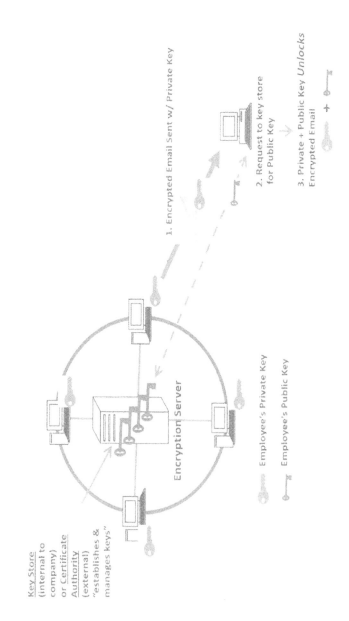

**Two-factor Authentication (2FA) – Asymmetric Cryptography
Basic Description**

External Certification Authority Program (ECA)

In the case of DOD, the ECA program affords businesses the ability to interface with its 2FA infrastructure. The ECA supports the issuing of DoD-approved certificates to industry partners and other external third-party entities and organizations. The ECA program is designed to provide vendors with the mechanism to securely communicate with the DoD and authenticate them to DoD Information Systems. It is expected to be further leveraged by other federal agencies as CMMC and NIST 800-171 requirements expand beyond DOD.

For new vendors, the following instructions should be helpful when the ECA requirement becomes mandatory. To obtain a Public Key Infrastructure (PKI) ECA Medium Assurance Certificate (MAC) will most likely be accomplished by two current significant vendors. The two vendors are: Either through the **Operational Research Consultants, Inc. (ORC)** at https://eca.orc.com/ or IdenTrust http://www.identrust.com/certificates/eca/index.html). The certificate will come in three forms: Software (browser-based), token (preloaded USB device), or hardware (CAC card loaded).

The cost ranges from $100-$300 and is suitable for one to three years, depending on the selected option. When visiting these sites, ensure that the correct certificate is chosen. Select the "ECA/Identity certificate." On the IdenTrust website, look for the Medium Assurance Certificate.

The process will take from one to two weeks to receive the certificate. The certificate will be provided by email with instructions on how to download the certificate. Once the certificate is received, contact the Contract Office to determine what help desk will need to be contacted to request account establishment on the respective federal IT infrastructure. It will typically require at least 30 minutes to 1 hour to create the account but expect longer with non-DOD federal agencies.

IdenTrust DOD ECA Program Site

SC.3.188

3.13.13 Control and monitor the use of mobile code.

MINIMUM/MORE COMPLETE ANSWER: Mobile code is mainly part of Internet-capable business phones. The company's phone carrier can limit the types and kinds of mobile applications that reside on employee phones. Most applications are usually required to meet secure industry development standards. It is best to confirm with the company's carrier how mobile code apps are secured and restrict employees to a set number of approved mobile apps. Define the base applications provided to each employee in the company procedures and the process for work-specific applications that other specialists in the company require.

SC.3.189

3.13.14 Control and monitor the use of Voice over Internet Protocol (VoIP) technologies.

MINIMUM ANSWER: The most likely current place VOIP would exist is the company's phone service. Ensure with the phone carrier that their VOIP services are secure and what security level is used to protect corporate communications. Furthermore, identify any contract information that provides details about the provided security.

MORE COMPLETE ANSWER: Verify what monitoring services and network protection (from malware, viruses, etc.) are part of the current service plan. If necessary, determine whether both the control and monitoring are included or extra services. If not fully covered, consider formulating a POAM. (See Appendix D: *Managing the Lifecycle of a POAM*).

SC.3.190

3.13.15 Protect the authenticity of communications sessions.
MINIMUM/ MORE COMPLETE ANSWER: This control addresses communications' protection and establishes confidence that the session is authentic; it ensures the individual's identity and the information being transmitted. Authenticity protection includes, for example, protecting against session hijacking or insertion of false information.

This can be resolved by some form, hard or soft token MFA/2FA, solution. It will ensure the identity and FIPS 140-2 encryption to prevent data manipulation. See Control 3.5.2 for further discussion. While these are not complete solutions, they significantly demonstrate more certainty that the communications are authentic.

SC.3.191

3.13.16 Protect the confidentiality of CUI[17] at rest.
MINIMUM ANSWER: This is a DAR issue, and as discussed earlier, it is a DOD requirement. Ensure the right software package is procured that meets FIPS 140-2 standards. (See Control 3.13.11 for NIST's website information).

MORE COMPLETE ANSWER: If using a CSP, ensure it uses DOD accepted FIPS 140-2 standards; it will make authorization simpler. Moreover, suppose the business cannot use FIPS 140-2 solutions. In that case, a reminder ensures an effective POAM is developed that addresses why it cannot be currently implemented and when the company is prepared to implement the control. *When will the company be compliant?*

---

[17] This also would include, FCI, and other public and private data deemed sensitive.

SC.3.192
(CMMC/CIS Controls)

SC.3.192: Implement Domain Name Service (DNS) filtering services.
MINIMUM /MORE COMPLETE ANSWER: Confirm with KO/CO or Program manager recommended DNS filtering services. Preferably execute as a cloud-based third-party managed service.

DNS Web Filtering: A service that filters based upon the Domain Name System (DNS) internet traffic. DNS Filtering will stop malicious sites from loading and prevent harmful content from affecting organizational networks and infrastructures. It is used to avoid viruses and malware. It typically relies upon *blacklists* to provide rules to prevent malicious sites from impacting operational capabilities.

SC.3.193
(CMMC-specific control)

SC.3.193: Implement a policy restricting the publication of CUI on publicly accessible websites (e.g., forums, LinkedIn, Facebook, Twitter, etc.)
MINIMUM/MORE COMPLETE ANSWER: Include restrictions of the publication of any CUI//FCI, etc., information from social media sites. Include disciplinary actions to include counseling or termination for cause.

SI.3.218
(CMMC-specific)

SI.3.218: Employ spam protection mechanisms at information system access entry and exit points.

MINIMUM ANSWER: Use **Managed access control** as described by NIST 800-171 security control, 3.1.14, described below.

MORE COMPLETE ANSWER: Employ **Virtual Private Network (VPN)** functionalities to reduce vulnerabilities to spam as described below.

Optional and Related NIST 800-171 Control

3.1.14 Route remote access via managed access control points.

MINIMUM ANSWER: **Managed access control** points are about control of traffic through "trusted" connections. For example, Verizon ® or AT&T® as the company's Internet Service Provider (ISP). It would be highly recommended to include any contracted services or Service Level Agreements (SLA)[18] from these providers. They may consist of additional threat and spam filtering services that could reduce the "bad guys" from gaining access to corporate data; these are ideal artifacts for proof of satisfactorily meeting this control.

MORE COMPLETE ANSWER: Another addition could also be using a **Virtual Private Network (VPN).** These are also common services the significant providers have for additional costs.

Describing and providing such agreements to DOD could also identify a **defense in depth** approach; the first level is through the VPN service. The second would be provided by the remote access software providing an additional layer of defense. Defense in depth can include such protective efforts to prevent unauthorized access to company IT assets:

- Physical protection (e.g., alarms, guards)

---

[18] See the latest version of "**The Cloud Service Level Agreement (CSLA): A Supplement for NIST 800-171 Implementation**" on Amazon for more information about the CSLA when seeking to deploy part or all of the corporate IT environment with a Cloud Service Provider (CSP).

- Perimeter (e.g., firewalls, Intrusion Detection System (IDS), "Trusted Internet Connections")
- Application/Executables (e.g., **whitelisting** of authorized software, **blacklisting** blocking specified programs)
- Data (e.g., Data Loss Protection programs, Access controls, auditing).

SI.3.219
(CMMC-specific)

SI.3.219: Implement email forgery protections.

MINIMUM/MORE COMPLETE ANSWER: Recommend the use of asymmetric email and digital signature services because of their everyday use within the DOD. It further affords compatibility with DOD security processes and procedures. Its implementation may be done directly or by using managed services as described below in optional NIST 800-171 control, 3.13.10.

Optional and Related NIST 800-171 Control

3.13.10 Establish and manage cryptographic keys for cryptography employed in the information system.

MINIMUM ANSWER: There are two significant scenarios likely to occur:

1. The use of commercial cryptographic programs that resides within the company's architecture or is provided by an external "managed service" provider is the most likely scenario. The keys will be maintained and secured by the cryptographic application. The company is establishing some form of 2FA solution. The public key would be acquired somewhere else in the architecture, and the private key that of the employee would reside on a token such as a CAC card or another critical device.

2. Using a DOD or other like 2FA solution with a CAC, Personal Identity Verification (PIV) card, or "token" such as those produced by RSA ® is likely if DOD authorizes the exchange of keys on its systems with that of the company. This requires a Certificate Authority (CA) usually outside the local network either managed by DOD or another trusted commercial entity with the capability to support "asymmetric" 2FA.

Whichever solution is used, ensure compatibility with DOD systems and other companies as part of its normal operations. **All transmittal of CUI//FCI data is required to be encrypted.**

MORE COMPLETE ANSWER: Any more exceptional ability to secure and protect the **company's key store** or through defined SLA's with outside service providers is essential. Ensure they have safeguards in place to protect unauthorized access to its system. They may use stronger encryption methods, but ensure they are recognized by DOD and are Federal Information Processing Standards (FIPS 140-2) compliant. (See NIST 800-171 Control 3.13.11 for identifying FIPS 140-2 solutions).

SI.3.220
(CIS Controls)

SI.3.220: Utilize email sandboxing to detect or block potentially malicious email attachments.

MINIMUM/MORE COMPLETE ANSWER: "sandboxing" places all email traffic into a separate IT environment to apply such tools as anti-virus and anti-malware detection tools. It is best to identify a Managed Service Provider (MSP) that may also be included as part of a company's ISP's services; this may also be an extended cost. It should be considered part of cybersecurity costs that may be billable back to the federal government.

Copyright 2021, Cybersentinel, LLC, All Rights Reserved
Washington, DC ∞ Tucson, AZ

CUI Classification, Marking & Storage Guide

Proper Marking of CUI[19]

Security markings and safeguarding are a significant part of being successful in the application of the CMMC. Proper marking is not just for the company or agency but for those not intended or authorized to view CUI. This chapter delineates how to mark all forms of written and electronic media to protect sensitive CUI. While it is unlikely a company or business will create CUI, it will be responsible for the legal protections from either administrative, civil, or criminal implications of failing to care for CUI properly. **Do not be careless.**

The CUI Program standardizes how the Executive branch handles unclassified information[20] that does not meet the criteria required for classification under E.O. 13526, "Classified National Security Information," December 29, 2009, Atomic Energy Act but must be protected based on law, regulation, or Government-wide policy. Protections involve the safeguards employed while this information is stored or handled by the Executive branch departments or subordinate agencies.

Before implementing the CUI Program, agencies employed *ad hoc*, agency-specific policies, procedures, and markings to safeguard and control this information. This information involved privacy, security, proprietary business interests, and law enforcement information. This was highly inefficient and confusing. Subsequent guidance resulted in inconsistent marking and safeguarding of documents that led to unclear or unnecessarily restrictive dissemination policies. Furthermore, it created obstacles to the *best practice* principle of *Information Sharing*, resulting in part from the 9-11 attack of September 11, 2001[21].

---

[19] This chapter is adapted from the National Archives and Records Administration (NARA) information and artifacts regarding the national CUI program.

[20] While the Legislative and Judicial Branch should defer to the Executive Branch for all matters regarding national security protections and markings, it cannot be guaranteed for vendors working with the other two branches of the US government.

[21] One of the major findings of the 9-11 Commission was that the Central Intelligence Agency (CIA) and the Federal Bureau of Investigation (FBI) each had pieces of critical intelligence that may have prevented the attacks. Congress mandated created information sharing efforts—however, the parochial nature of government has not as of yet solved this problem.

Proper markings alert information holders to the presence of CUI and subsequently when portion markings are required. Markings ensure that CUI is identified and the exact information is appropriately marked for protection. They alert CUI holders to any dissemination and safeguarding controls. This chapter provides basic marking guidelines for CUI and is written to give visibility and requisite security to CUI.

Companies, businesses, organizations, agencies, and most specifically, employees must review their organizations' CUI policy before marking any CUI. The handling of CUI must be per **E.O. 13556, "Controlled Unclassified Information," November 4, 2010**, 32 CFR Part 2002 (this link provides a full version https://www.govinfo.gov/content/pkg/CFR-2017-title32-vol6/pdf/CFR-2017-title32-vol6-part2002.pdf), supplemental guidance published by the government's overall CUI Executive Agent (EA), the National Archive and Records Administration (NARA), and all applicable EA-approved agency policies. This chapter contains guidance on what each marking is, where and how to apply it, and which items are mandatory or optional based on local agency or organization policy.

CUI Banner Markings (Reference 32 CFR 2002.20(b))

Banner markings are the necessary header (and footer) designations alerting individuals with a need-to-know the mandatory restrictions to ensure the protection of the information. Individuals should see banner makings to provide maximum security if the information is set out in the open or inadvertently visible to unauthorized individuals. Those individuals charged with the CUI protection are administratively responsible for CUI and security and are subject to disciplinary actions by the agency or company. The following is a list of basic knowledge required by the agency and recipient vendors and contractors of the US Government.

- The initial marking for all CUI is the CUI Banner Marking. This is the central marking that appears at the top (and typically, at the bottom) of each page of any document that contains CUI.

- This marking is MANDATORY for all documents containing CUI. The CUI Banner Marking content must be inclusive of all CUI within the text and must be the same on each page.

- The Banner Marking should appear as bold capitalized black text and be centered when feasible. (*There are no designated size or font requirements, but we recommend the same font used for the document and at least four sizes larger for visual prominence*).
- The CUI Banner Marking may include up to three elements:

    1. The CUI Control Marking (mandatory) may consist of either the word "CONTROLLED" or the acronym "CUI."

    2. CUI Category or Subcategory Markings (mandatory for CUI Specified). These are separated from the CUI Control Marking by a double forward-slash (//). When including multiple categories or subcategories in a Banner Marking, they must be alphabetized and are separated by a single forward-slash (/).

    3. A double forward-slash precedes limited Dissemination (LIMDIS) Control Markings (//) to separate them from the rest of the CUI Banner Marking.

A sample of the CUI Banner Marking may be found below.

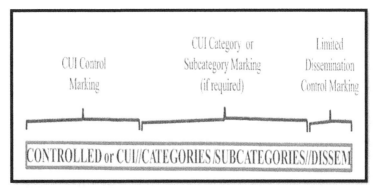

CUI Banner Marking

The above example uses the words "CATEGORIES" and "SUBCATEGORIES" as substitutes for CUI Category or Subcategory Markings and the word "DISSEM" as a substitute for Limited Dissemination Control Marking. Consult the CUI Registry for actual CUI markings.

CUI Banner Control Markings (Reference 32 CFR 2002.20(b)(1))

The CUI Control Marking is mandatory for all CUI and may consist of either the word "CONTROLLED" or the acronym "CUI" (at the designator's discretion). A best practice for CUI Banner Marking includes it being placed at the bottom of the document. Below are two examples showing the options for the CUI Banner Marking.

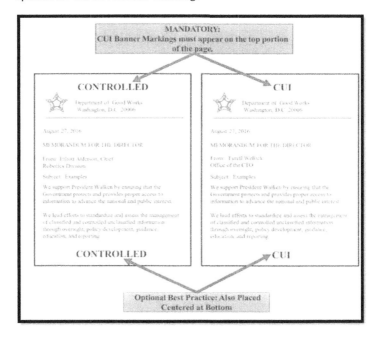

CUI Categories and Subcategories (Reference 32 CFR 2002.12)

The CUI Program is founded on the precondition that only information requiring protection based on law, Federal regulation, or government-wide policy can qualify as CUI. *CUI Categories and Subcategories are necessarily different*. CUI Categories and Subcategories are based on at least one or more laws, regulations, or government-wide policies; these are also referred to as *Authorities*[22] that

---

[22] Consider Authorities as local rules or policies that are unique to the particular Federal agency. Typically, the Contract Officer should be able to assist in information briefings with the agency to ensure full compliance by the vendor.

require a specific type of information to be protected or restricted in its dissemination.

There are two types of CUI Categories and Subcategories: CUI Basic and CUI Specified.

1. ***CUI Basic*** is the standard CUI category. All rules of CUI apply to CUI Basic Categories and Subcategories. This ensures the proper creation and handling of properly marked CUI.

2. ***CUI Specified*** is different since the requirements for how users must treat each type of information vary with each Category or Subcategory. This is because some Authorities have specialized needs for handling varied kinds of CUI information.

CUI Specified is NOT a "higher level" of CUI. It is *merely different*. Its differences are dictated by law, Federal regulation, or government-wide policy; they cannot be ignored. Furthermore, a document containing multiple CUI Specified Categories and Subcategories must include all of them in the CUI Banner Marking.

There is one additional issue with CUI Specified. Some CUI Categories and Subcategories are only CUI Specified, sometimes based upon the Authorities' local rules or policies. These differences are caused by differing laws or regulations about the same information type; however, only *some* of them may include additional or alternate handling requirements for standard CUI Basic.

Therefore, only CUI created under Authorities would be CUI Specified. Explicitly, suppose the law, regulation, or Government-wide policy that pertains to an agency are listed in the CUI Registry as a Specified Authority. In that case, you must mark the CUI based on that Authority as CUI Specified and include that marking in the CUI Banner.

The CUI Registry may be found at https://www.archives.gov/cui/registry/category-list

Banner Markings for Category and Subcategory Markings (Reference 32 CFR 2002.20(b)(2))

    A double forward-slash separates CUI Category or Subcategory Markings (//) from the CUI Control Marking. When including multiple CUI Category or Subcategory Markings in the CUI Banner Marking, they must be separated by a single forward-slash (/). When a document contains CUI Specified, all CUI Specified Category or Subcategory Markings must be included in the CUI Banner Marking.

    Additionally, agency heads may approve the use of CUI Basic Category or Subcategory Markings through agency CUI policy. When such agency policy exists, all CUI Basic Category or Subcategory Markings must be included in the CUI Banner Marking.

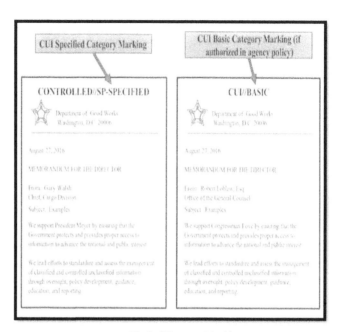

Varied Banner Markings

The above examples use the words "SP-SPECIFIED" and "BASIC" as substitutes for CUI Category and Subcategory Markings. Consult the CUI Registry for actual CUI markings.

Since CUI Specified Categories and Subcategories are different – both from CUI Basic and from each other – CUI Specified MUST always be included in the CUI Banner. This is done to ensure that every authorized CUI holder and end-user who receives a document containing CUI Specified knows that the document must be treated in a manner that differs from CUI Basic. This is accomplished in two ways:

1. All CUI Specified documents must include the Category or Subcategory marking for all the CUI Specified in that document in the CUI Banner Marking. This ensures that initially, a user in receipt of that document is aware of the CUI Banner. This permits the user to be mindful of whether they have something other than ordinary CUI Basic. It also allows the user to meet any additional or alternative requirements for the CUI Specified they hold.

2. To ensure that it is evident that a Category or Subcategory is Specified, the marking has "SP-" added to the beginning of the marking after the CUI or Controlled designation.

The above examples use the word "SPECIFIED" as a substitute for CUI Category and Subcategory Markings. Consult the CUI Registry for actual CUI markings.

Banner Markings with Multiple of Subcategory Markings (Reference 32 CFR 2002.20)

CUI Specified Markings must precede CUI Basic Markings authorized for use by the agency head in the CUI Banner. Consult the agency CUI policy for guidance on the use of CUI Basic Category or Subcategory Markings. Additionally, CUI Category and Subcategory Markings MUST be alphabetized within CUI type (Basic or Specified).

Alphabetized Specified CUI categories and subcategories must precede alphabetized Basic CUI categories and subcategories.

Below are examples of CUI Banner Markings used in a document that contains both CUI Specified and CUI Basic.

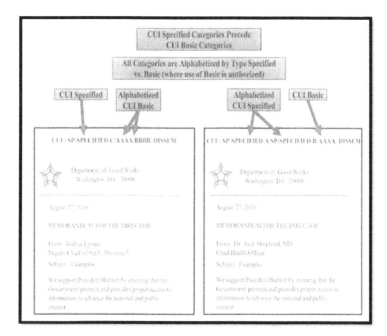

Multiple Category or Subcategory Markings

The above examples use "AAAA" and "BBBB" as substitutes for CUI Basic Category and Subcategory Markings, "SP-SPECIFIED-X" as a substitute for a CUI Specified Category and Subcategory Markings, and "DISSEM" as a substitute for a Limited Dissemination Control Marking. Consult the CUI Registry for actual CUI markings.

Banner Markings (Limited Dissemination Controls)(Reference 32 CFR 2002.20(b)(3)

Only Limited Dissemination (LIMDIS) Control Markings found in the CUI Registry are authorized for CUI. Limited Dissemination Control

Markings are separated from preceding sections of the CUI Banner Marking by double forward-slash (///). When a document contains multiple Limited Dissemination Control Markings, those Limited Dissemination Control Markings MUST be alphabetized and separated from each other with a single forward-slash (/).

Below are examples that show the proper use of Limited Dissemination Control Markings in the CUI Banner Marking in a letter-type document or a slide presentation.

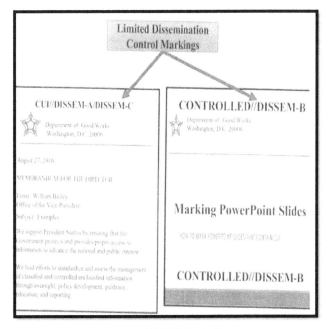

LIMDIS Controls

The above example uses "DISSEM-X" as a substitute for Limited Dissemination Control Markings. Consult the CUI Registry for actual CUI markings.

Designation Indicator (Reference 32 CFR 2002.20(a)(3)(d))

All documents containing CUI must indicate the designator's agency. This may be accomplished with letterhead, a signature block with the agency, or the use of a "Controlled by" line. Every effort should be made to identify a point of contact, branch, or division within an organization responsible for either creating or protecting the CUI.

Below are examples of Designation Indicators in a slide presentation and a letter-type document.

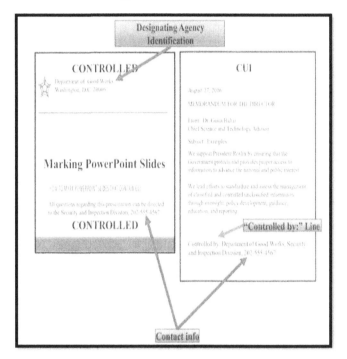

Designation Indicators

Portion Markings (Reference 32 CFR 2002.20(f))

Portion marking of CUI is *optional* in a fully unclassified document but is highly encouraged[23] to facilitate information sharing and proper handling. Agency heads may approve the required use of CUI Portion marking on all CUI generated within their agency. Users

---

[23] The author strongly supports the use of portion markings. They further help when providing reports and responding to requests for information from the public; this provides clear boundaries for information release in accordance with the law.

should always consult their agency's CUI policy when creating CUI documents.

When CUI Portion Marking is used, these rules will be followed. CUI Portion Markings are placed at the beginning of the portion (e.g., beginning of sentence or segment of the CUI), apply throughout the entire document. CUI Portion Markings are contained within parentheses and may include up to three elements:

1. The CUI Control Marking: This is mandatory when portion marking and must be the acronym "CUI" (the word "Controlled" will not be used in portion marking).
2. CUI Category or Subcategory Markings: These can be found in the CUI Registry.
    a. When used, CUI Category or Subcategory Markings are separated from the CUI Control Marking by a double forward-slash (//).
    b. When including multiple categories or subcategories in a portion, CUI Category or Subcategory Markings are separated by a single forward-slash (/).
3. Limited Dissemination Control Markings: These can be found in the CUI Registry and are separated from preceding CUI markings by a double forward-slash (//). When including multiple Limited Dissemination Control Markings, they must be alphabetized and separated from each other by a single forward-slash (/).
4. When CUI Portion Markings are used, and a portion does not contain CUI, a "U" is placed in parentheses to indicate that the portion includes Uncontrolled Unclassified Information.

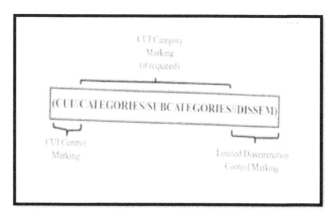

Portion Marking Standards

The above example uses the words "CATEGORIES" and "SUBCATEGORIES" as substitutes for CUI Category or Subcategory Markings and the word "DISSEM" as a substitute for a Limited Dissemination Control Marking. Consult the CUI Registry for actual CUI markings.

The presence of at least one item categorized as CUI in a document requires CUI marking of the entire document. CUI Portion Markings can be of significant assistance in determining if a document contains CUI and, therefore, must be marked appropriately. Additionally, when portion markings are used, and any portion does not include CUI, a "(U)" is placed in front of that portion to indicate that it has Uncontrolled or non-CUI -Unclassified[24] Information.

---

[24] Uncontrolled appears to be an ambiguous stamen from NARA; it is best considered as UNCLASSIFIED information that can be freely shared with the general public.

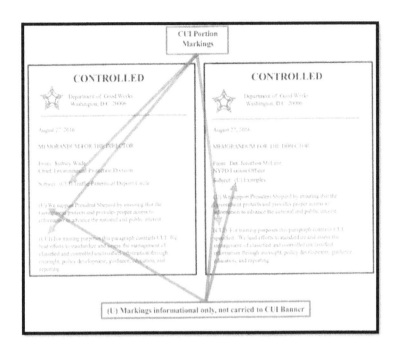

"Parenthetical" Portion Marking Examples

Portion Markings with Category Only (Reference 32 CFR 2002.20(f))

This example shows how to portion mark a document using the CUI Control Marking and CUI Category or Subcategory Markings. When a document contains CUI Specified, all CUI Specified Category or Subcategory Markings must be included in the CUI Banner Marking. Consult your agency CUI policy for guidance on the use of CUI Basic Category or Subcategory Markings. When CUI Portion Markings are used, and a portion does not contain CUI, a "U" is placed in parentheses to indicate that the portion includes Uncontrolled-Unclassified Information.

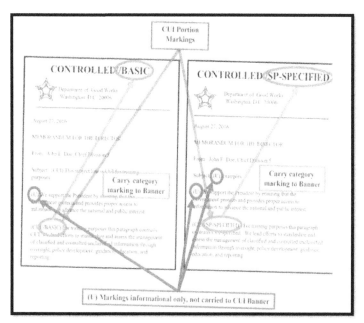

Portion Marking with Category Only

The above example uses "BASIC" and "SPECIFIED" as substitutes for CUI Category or Subcategory Markings. Consult the CUI Registry for actual CUI markings.

Portion Markings with Category and Dissemination Caveats (Reference 32 CFR 2002.20(f))

The example below shows how to portion mark a document using all three CUI Banner Marking components. When a document contains CUI Specified, CUI Specified Category or Subcategory Markings must be included in the CUI Banner Marking. Consult your agency CUI policy for guidance on the use of CUI Basic Category or Subcategory Markings. Also, when CUI Portion Markings are used, and a portion does not contain CUI, a "U" is placed in parentheses to indicate that the portion includes Uncontrolled-Unclassified Information.

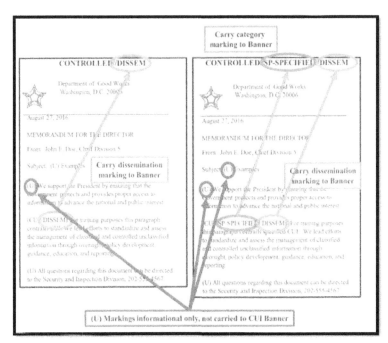

Portion Markings with Category and Dissemination

The above example uses "SP-SPECIFIED" as a substitute for a CUI Category or Subcategory Marking and "DISSEM" as a substitute for Limited Dissemination Control Markings. Consult the CUI Registry for actual CUI markings.

Common Mistakes in Banner Markings

Category and Subcategory Markings for CUI Specified MUST always be included in the Banner Marking, and those for CUI Basic may be required by agency CUI policy. When CUI Portion Markings are used and have CUI Category or Subcategory Markings, those markings MUST be included in the CUI Banner Marking.

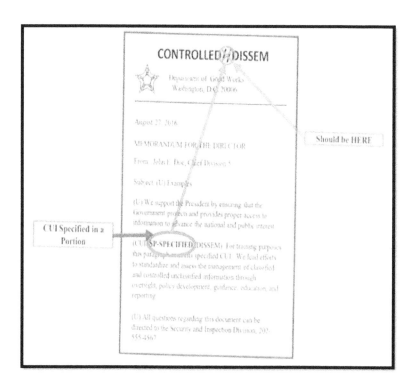

The above example uses "SP-SPECIFIED" as a substitute for a CUI Specified Category or Subcategory Marking and "DISSEM" as a substitute for a Limited Dissemination Control Marking. Consult the CUI Registry for actual CUI markings.

Marking of Multiple Pages (Reference 32 CFR 2002.20(c))

The CUI Banner Marking composition for a multi-page document is essentially the totality of all the CUI markings in the document; if any portion of the document contains CUI Specified or a Limited Dissemination Control Marking, then the CUI Banner Marking must reflect that.

Below is an example of one multi-page document with CUI Portion Marking.

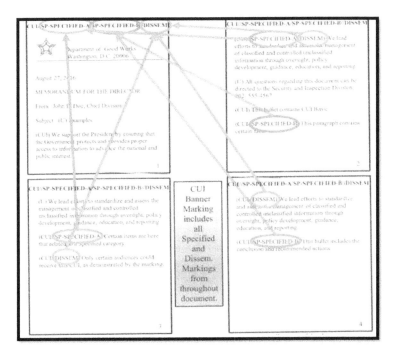

The overall CUI Banner Marking for the document must appear on all pages of the document.

Required Indicators as directed by Authorities (Reference 32 CFR 2002.20 (b)(2)(iii))

Required indicators that include informational, warning, or dissemination statements may be mandated by the law, Federal regulation, or Government-wide policy that makes a specific item of information CUI. These indicators shall not be included in the CUI Banner or portion markings but must appear in a manner readily apparent to authorized personnel. This shall be consistent with the requirements of the governing document.

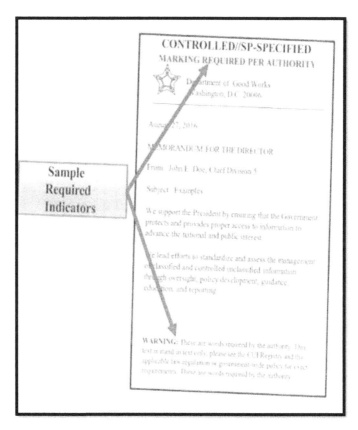

The above example uses "SPECIFIED" as a substitute for a CUI Specified Category or Subcategory Marking. Consult the CUI Registry for actual CUI markings.

Supplemental Administrative Markings (Reference 32 CFR 2002.20(l))

Agencies may use supplemental administrative markings (e.g., Draft, Deliberative, Pre- decisional, Provisional) along with CUI to inform recipients of the non-final status of documents ONLY when such markings are created and defined in agency policy.

Supplemental administrative markings may not be used to control CUI and may not be commingled with or incorporated into the CUI Banner Marking or Portion Markings. Additional administrative markings may not duplicate any marking in the CUI Registry.

Below are two examples of ways to properly use additional administrative markings.

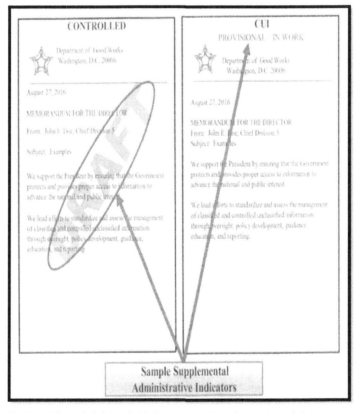

Common Mistakes for Supplemental Administrative Markings

Supplemental administrative markings may not be used to control CUI. They must not be incorporated into CUI Banner Markings or CUI Portion Markings or duplicate any marking in the CUI Registry.

Below are two examples of ways **NOT** to use administrative markings.

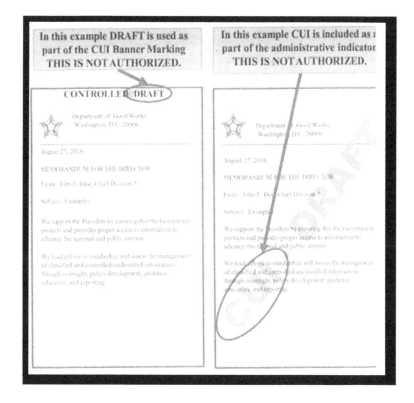

Electronic Media Storage and Marking Procedures (Reference 32 CFR 2002.20)

Media such as USB sticks, hard drives, and CD ROMs must be marked to alert CUI holders to the presence of CUI stored on the device. Due to space limitations, it may not be possible to include Category, Subcategory, or Limited Dissemination Control Markings on the given surface. At a minimum, mark media with the CUI Control Marking ("CONTROLLED" or "CUI") and the Designating Agency. Equipment can be marked or labeled to indicate that CUI is stored on the device.

Removable Hard drive

Equipment can be marked or labeled to indicate that CUI is stored on the device

NOTE: DOGW is an acronym for Department of Good Works.

Marking Forms (Reference 32 CFR 2002.20)

Forms that contain CUI must be marked when completed. If space on the form is limited, cover sheets can be used for this purpose. As forms are updated during agency implementation of the CUI Program, they should be modified to include a statement that indicates the form is CUI when finalized.

CUI Coversheets (Reference 32 CFR 2002.32)

The use of CUI coversheets is optional except when required by agency policy. Agencies may download coversheets from the CUI Registry or obtain printed copies through the General Services Administration (GSA) Global Supply Centers or the GSAAdvantage online service (https://www.gsa.gov/buying-selling/purchasing-programs/requisition-programs/gsa-global-supply/easy-ordering/gsa-global-supply-online-ordering).

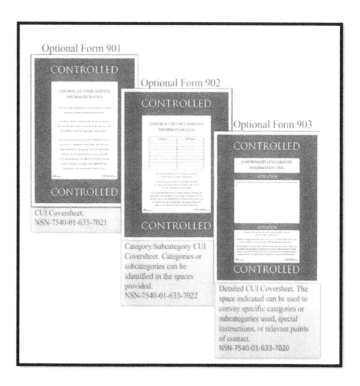

Marking Transmittal Documents (Reference 32 CFR 2002.20)

When a transmittal document accompanies CUI, the transmittal document must indicate that CUI is attached or enclosed. The transmittal document must also include, conspicuously, the following or similar instructions, as appropriate:

- "When the enclosure is removed, this document is Uncontrolled- Unclassified Information"; or
- "When the enclosure is removed, this document is (CUI Control Level); or
- "Upon removal, this document does not contain CUI."

Alternate Marking Methods (Reference 32 CFR 2002.20)

Agency heads[25] may authorize alternate marking methods on IT systems, websites, browsers, or databases through agency CUI policy. These may be used to alert users to the presence of CUI, where the agency head has issued a limited CUI marking waiver for CUI designated within the agency. These warnings may take multiple forms and include the examples below.

---

[25] Agency Heads may be considered federal agency secretaries, leadership, etc., designated under contract to provide direct oversight of the agencies' CUI program.

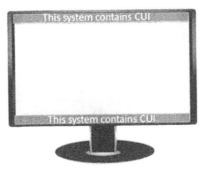

Computer Monitor CUI Banners

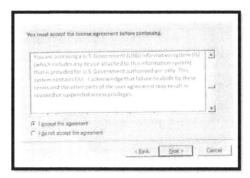

Agency or Company Legal Warning Notification

Room or Area Markings (Reference 32 CFR 2002.20)

In areas containing CUI, it may be necessary to alert personnel who cannot access the site or information. This may be accomplished by any means approved by the agency and detailed in its CUI policy. Typically, signs are posted exterior to the room or rooms, on all entry doors, and in any ante-room designated to verify clearances or need-to-know status of a group or individual.

Below is a sample of a sign that indicates CUI is present.

Example Exterior Door and Interior Rooms Sign

Container Markings (Reference 32 CFR 2002.20)

When an agency is storing CUI, authorized holders should mark the container to indicate CUI.

Below are some basic examples.

Shipping and Mailing (Reference 32 CFR 2002.20)

Agency heads must ensure that mailroom staff is trained in handling CUI to include reporting any loss, theft, or misuse.

When shipping CUI:

- Address packages that contain CUI for delivery only to a specific recipient.
- DO NOT put CUI markings on the outside of an envelope or package for mailing/shipping.
- Use in-transit automated tracking and accountability tools where possible.

Re-marking Legacy Information (Reference 32 CFR 2002.36)

Legacy information is unclassified information that was marked as restricted from access or dissemination in some way or otherwise controlled before the CUI Program was established. **All legacy information is not automatically CUI.** Agencies must examine and determine what legacy information qualifies as CUI and mark it accordingly.

In cases of excessive burden, an agency's head may issue a "Legacy Marking Waiver," as described in 32 CFR 2002.38(b) of the CUI Rule. When the agency head grants such a waiver, legacy material that qualifies need not be re-marked as CUI until and unless it is to be "re-used" in a new document.

> # LEGACY MARKING
>
> Department of Good Works
> Washington, D.C. 20006
>
> ---
>
> August 27, 2016
>
> MEMORANDUM FOR THE DIRECTOR
>
> From: John E. Doe, Chief Division 5
>
> Subject: Examples
>
> We support the President by ensuring that the Government protects and provides proper access to information to advance the national and public interest.
>
> We lead efforts to standardize and assess the management of classified and controlled unclassified information through oversight, policy development, guidance, education, and reporting.

"LEGACY MARKING" is used as a substitute for ad hoc, agency markings used to label unclassified information before creating the CUI Program.

When legacy information is to be re-used and incorporated into another document of any kind, it must undergo the process described below.

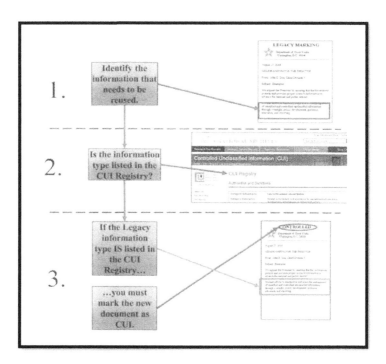

When possible, contact the originator of the information for guidance in remarking and protecting the CUI Program's legacy information.

CUI Markings in a Classified Environment

Marking Commingled Information (Reference 32 CFR 2002.20(g))

When CUI is included in a document that contains any classified information, that document is referred to as ***commingled***. Commingled documents are subject to the CUI and Classified National Security Information (CNSI) programs' requirements. As a best practice, keep the CUI and classified information in separate and designated areas to the greatest extent possible[26]. Mark all portions to ensure that authorized holders can distinguish CUI portions from those containing CNSI or Uncontrolled-Unclassified Information; the de-controlling provisions for CUI apply only to portions marked as CUI. CNSI portions remain classified to their declassification requirements.

Executive Order 13526 - Classified National Security Information

In the overall marking banner's CUI section, double forward slashes (//) are used to separate significant elements, and single forward slashes (/) are used to separate sub-elements. The CUI Control Marking ("CUI") appears in the overall banner marking

---

[26] Typically, classified facilities should be partitioned to include designated drawers, safes, and folders specific to CUI storage.

directly before the CUI category and subcategory markings. CUI Specified in the document, CUI Specified category, and subcategory marking(s) must appear in the overall banner marking. Per agency policy, if used, the optional CUI Basic category and subcategory markings would appear next. Both CUI Specified and CUI Basic markings are separately alphabetized. The limited dissemination control markings apply to the entire document and the CUI and classified information in it. Placeholders are not used for missing elements or sub-elements.

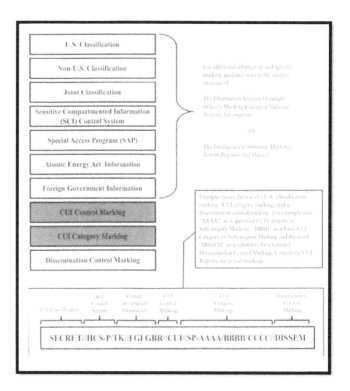

Commingling in the same paragraph is not recommended. Where sections contain CUI and CNSI commingled, portion marking elements follow a similar syntax to the banner marking. <u>However, the paragraph always takes the HIGHEST classification of the information contained in the section.</u>

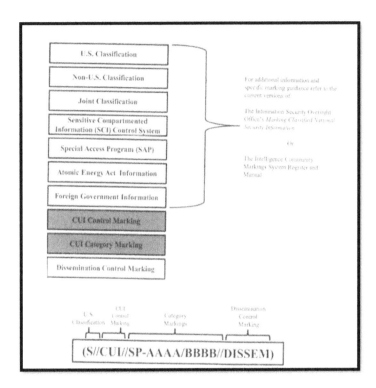

For additional information and specific marking, the guidance refers to the current versions of The Information Security Oversight Office's *Marking Classified National Security Information*.

Commingling Example 1

In cases where CUI is commingled with classified information, the following applies:

- In banners, the CUI Control Marking is used only in its abbreviated form ("CUI"). The longer form ("CONTROLLED") is not used. Either the classification marking, CUI control marking ("CUI"), or the Uncontrolled Unclassified Marking ("U") must be used in every portion.

- Limited Dissemination Control Markings must appear in the banner line and in all portions to which they apply.

Best practice: CUI and CNSI should be placed in separate portions of a document.

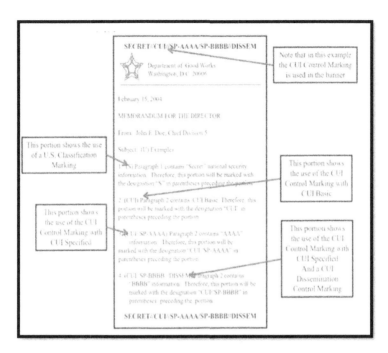

The above examples use "SP-AAAA" or "SP-BBBB" as CUI Specified Category or Subcategory Markings and the word "DISSEM" as a substitute for a Limited Dissemination Control Marking. Consult the CUI Registry for actual markings.

Commingling Example 2

These examples show the various ways CUI may be identified in a document.

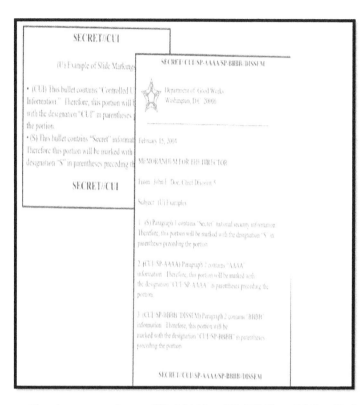

The above examples use "SP-AAAA" or "SP-BBBB" as CUI Specified Category or Subcategory Markings and the word "DISSEM" as a substitute for a Limited Dissemination Control Marking. Consult the CU Registry for actual markings.

Commingling Example 3

Below are two CUI samples commingled with classified information, specifically with Classified National Security Information (CNSI). The sample on the left has the CUI and CNSI broken into separate paragraphs allowing for more natural future separation when needed to accommodate differing access requirements. The example on the right has CUI and CNSI in the same paragraph.

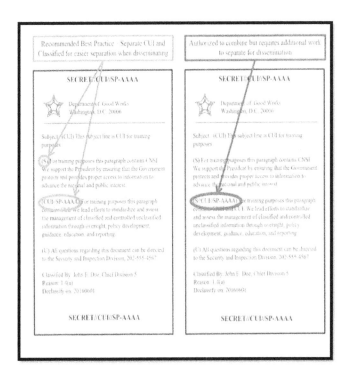

The above examples use the word "SP-AAAA" as a substitute for a CUI Specified Category or Subcategory Marking. Consult the CUI Registry for actual markings.

Commingling Portion Markings (Reference 32 CFR 2002.20(g))

When a portion contains both CUI and classified information in a commingled document, the portion marking for the classified information must precede the CUI Portion Marking. When commingling CUI with classified information, the user should retain the CUI and classified portions separate to the greatest extent possible to allow for maximum information sharing. Many of the intricate markings seen below can be avoided by following this simple practice. Below are some examples of how to mark portions containing CUI.

Portion Marking	Contents of Portions Marked Section – CUI ONLY IN PORTION
(CUI)	This section contains CUI Basic.
(CUI/AAAA)	This section contains CUI Basic (with optional category marking).
(CUI/SP-BBBB)	This section contains CUI Specified.
(CUI/SP-BBBB/SP-CCCC)	This section contains two CUI Specified Categories in alphabetical order.
(CUI/DISSEM)	This section contains CUI Basic with a Limited Dissemination Control Marking
(CUI/AAAA//DISSEM)	This section contains CUI Basic with a Limited Dissemination Control Marking
(CUI/SP-BBBB//DISSEM)	This section contains CUI Specified with a Limited Dissemination Control Marking.
Portion Marking	Contents of Portions Marked Section – WITH COMMINGLED PORTIONS (NOT RECOMMENDED)
(S//CUI)	This section contains Secret information and CUI Basic.
(S//CUI/AAAA)	This section contains Secret information and CUI Basic (with optional category marking).
(S//CUI/SP-BBBB)	This section contains Secret information and CUI Specified.
(S//CUI/SP-BBBB/SP-CCCC)	This section contains Secret information and contains two CUI Specified Categories in alphabetical order.
(S//CUI/SP-BBBB//DISSEM)	This section contains Secret information and CUI Specified with a Limited Dissemination Control Marking.

Appendices

APPENDIX A -- RELEVANT REFERENCES

Federal Information Security Modernization Act of 2014 (P.L. 113-283), December 2014.
http://www.gpo.gov/fdsys/pkg/PLAW-113publ283/pdf/PLAW-113publ283.pdf

Executive Order 13556, *Controlled Unclassified Information*, November 2010.
http://www.gpo.gov/fdsys/pkg/FR-2010-11-09/pdf/2010-28360.pdf

Executive Order 13636, *Improving Critical Infrastructure Cybersecurity*, February 2013.
http://www.gpo.gov/fdsys/pkg/FR-2013-02-19/pdf/2013-03915.pdf

National Institute of Standards and Technology Federal Information Processing Standards
Publication 200 (as amended), *Minimum Security Requirements for Federal Information
and Information Systems*.
http://csrc.nist.gov/publications/fips/fips200/FIPS-200-final-march.pdf

National Institute of Standards and Technology Special Publication 800-53 (as amended),
Security and Privacy Controls for Federal Information Systems and Organizations.
http://dx.doi.org/10.6028/NIST.SP.800-53r4

National Institute of Standards and Technology Special Publication 800-171, rev. 1,
Protecting Controlled Unclassified Information in Nonfederal Information Systems and Organizations.
https://nvlpubs.nist.gov/nistpubs/SpecialPublications/NIST.SP.800-171r1.pdf

National Institute of Standards and Technology Special Publication 800-171A,
Assessing Security Requirements for Controlled Unclassified Information
https://csrc.nist.gov/CSRC/media/Publications/sp/800-171a/draft/sp800-171A-draft.pdf

National Institute of Standards and Technology *Framework for Improving Critical Infrastructure Cybersecurity* (as amended).
http://www.nist.gov/cyberframework

APPENDIX B -- TERMS & GLOSSARY

Audit log. A chronological record of information system activities, including records of system accesses and operations performed in a given period.

Authentication. Verifying a user's identity, process, or device is often a prerequisite to allowing access to resources in an information system.

Availability. Ensuring timely and reliable access to and use of information.

Baseline Configuration. A documented set of specifications for an information system, or a configuration item within a system, has been formally reviewed and agreed on at a given point in time, which can be changed only through change control procedures.

Blacklisting. The process used to identify: (i) software programs that are not authorized to execute on an information system; or (ii) prohibited websites.

Confidentiality. Preserving authorized restrictions on information access and disclosure, including means for protecting personal privacy and proprietary information.

Configuration Management. A collection of activities focused on establishing and maintaining the integrity of information technology products and information systems through control of processes for initializing, changing, and monitoring those products and systems' configurations throughout the system development life cycle.

Controlled Unclassified Information (CUI).
Information that law, regulation, or governmentwide policy requires to have safeguarding or disseminating controls, excluding information classified under Executive Order 13526, Classified National Security Information, December 29, 2009, or any predecessor or successor order, or the Atomic Energy Act of 1954, as amended.

External network. A network not controlled by the company.

FIPS-validated cryptography. A cryptographic module validated by the Cryptographic Module Validation Program (CMVP) meets the requirements specified in FIPS Publication 140-2 (as amended). As a prerequisite to CMVP validation, the cryptographic module must employ a cryptographic algorithm implementation that has successfully passed validation testing by the Cryptographic Algorithm Validation Program (CAVP).

Hardware. The physical components of an information system.

Incident. An occurrence that actually or potentially jeopardizes the confidentiality, integrity, or availability of an information system or the information the system processes, stores, or transmits or constitutes a violation or imminent threat of violation of security policies, security procedures, or acceptable use policies.

Information Security. The protection of information and information systems from unauthorized access, use, disclosure, disruption, modification, or destruction provides confidentiality, integrity, and availability.

Information System. A discrete set of information resources is organized to collect, process, maintain, use, share, disseminate, or dispense information.

Information Technology.	Any equipment or interconnected system or subsystem of equipment used in the automatic acquisition, storage, manipulation, management, movement, control, display, switching, interchange, transmission, or reception of data or information by the executive agency. It includes computers, ancillary equipment, software, firmware, similar procedures, services (including support services), and related resources.
Integrity.	Guarding against improper information modification or destruction and includes ensuring information non-repudiation and authenticity.
Internal Network.	A network where: (i) the establishment, maintenance, and provisioning of security controls are under the direct control of organizational employees or contractors; or (ii) cryptographic encapsulation or similar security technology implemented between organization-controlled endpoints provides the same effect (at least concerning confidentiality and integrity).
Malicious Code.	Software intended to perform an unauthorized process that will hurt the confidentiality, integrity, or availability of an information system; a virus, worm, Trojan horse, or other code-based entity that infects a host. Spyware and some forms of adware are also examples of malicious code.
Media.	Physical devices or writing surfaces include magnetic tapes, optical disks, magnetic disks, and printouts (but not including display media) onto which information is recorded, stored, or printed within an information system.
Mobile Code.	Software programs or parts of programs obtained from remote information systems, transmitted across a network, and executed on a local information system without explicit installation or execution by the recipient.

Mobile device. A portable computing device that: (i) has a small form factor such that a single individual can easily carry it; (ii) is designed to operate without a physical connection (e.g., wirelessly transmit or receive information); (iii) possesses local, non-removable or removable data storage; and (iv) includes a self-contained power source. Mobile devices may also have voice communication capabilities, on-board sensors that allow the devices to capture information, or build-in features to synchronize local data with remote locations. Examples include smartphones, tablets, and E-readers.

Multifactor Authentication. Authentication using two or more different factors to achieve authentication. Factors include: (i) something you know (e.g., password/PIN); (ii) something you have (e.g., cryptographic identification device, token); or (iii) something you are (e.g., biometric).

Nonfederal Information System. An information system that does not meet the criteria for a federal information system. Nonfederal organization.

Network. Information system(s) implemented with a collection of interconnected components. Such components may include routers, hubs, cabling, telecommunications controllers, key distribution centers, and technical control devices.

Portable storage device. An information system component that can be inserted into and removed from an information system is used to store data or information (e.g., text, video, audio, or image data). Such components are typically implemented on magnetic, optical, or solid-state devices (e.g., floppy disks, compact/digital video disks, flash/thumb drives, external hard disk drives, and flash memory cards/drives that contain nonvolatile memory).

Privileged Account.	An information system account with authorizations of a privileged user.
Privileged User.	A user who is authorized (and therefore, trusted) performs security-relevant functions that ordinary users cannot perform.
Remote Access.	Access to an organizational information system by a user (or a process acting on behalf of a user) communicating through an external network (e.g., the Internet).
Risk.	A measure of the extent to which a potential circumstance or event threatens an entity, and typically a function of (i) the adverse impacts that would arise if the situation or event occurs; and (ii) the likelihood of occurrence. Information system-related security risks are those risks that arise from the loss of confidentiality, integrity, or availability of information or information systems and reflect the potential adverse impacts to organizational operations (including mission, functions, image, or reputation), organizational assets, individuals, other organizations, and the Nation.
Sanitization.	Actions were taken to render data written on media unrecoverable by ordinary and, for some forms of sanitization, extraordinary means. The process of removing information from media such that data recovery is not possible. It includes removing all classified labels, markings, and activity logs.
Security Control.	A safeguard or countermeasure is prescribed for an information system or an organization designed to protect the confidentiality, integrity, and availability of its information and meet a set of defined security requirements.

Security Control Assessment. The testing or evaluation of security controls to determine the extent to which the controls are implemented correctly, operating as intended, and producing the desired outcome concerning meeting the security requirements for an information system or organization.

Security Functions. The hardware, software, or firmware of the information system responsible for enforcing the system security policy and supporting the isolation of code and data on which the protection is based.

Threat. Any circumstance or event with the potential to adversely impact organizational operations (including mission, functions, image, or reputation), organizational assets, individuals, other organizations, or the Nation through an information system via unauthorized access, destruction, disclosure, modification of information, or denial of service.

Whitelisting. The process used to identify: (i) software programs authorized to execute an information system.

APPENDIX C – CONTINUOUS MONITORING

NOTE: CM in this article is about Continuous Monitoring (ConMon) activities discussed in greater depth; it should not be confused with discussion in this book regarding Configuration Management.

Continuous Monitoring: A More Detailed Discussion

Cybersecurity is not about shortcuts. There are no easy solutions to years of leaders demurring their responsibility to address cyberspace's growing threats. We hoped that the Office of Personnel Management (OPM) breach several years ago would herald the needed focus, energy, and funding to quash the bad-guys. That has proven an empty hope where leaders have abrogated their responsibility to lead in cyberspace. The "holy grail" solution of Continuous Monitoring (CM) has been the most misunderstood solution. Too many shortcuts are perpetrated by numerous federal agencies and the private sector to create an illusion of success. This paper is specifically written to help leaders better understand what constitutes an accurate statement of: "we have continuous monitoring." This is not about shortcuts. This is about education, training, and understanding at the highest leadership levels that cybersecurity is not a technical issue but a leadership issue.

The Committee on National Security Systems defines CM as: "[t]he processes implemented to maintain current security status for one or more information systems on which the operational mission of the enterprise depends" (CNSS, 2010). CM has been described as the holistic solution of end-to-end cybersecurity coverage and the answer to providing an effective global Risk Management (RM) solution. It promises the elimination of the 3-year recertification cycle that has been the bane of cybersecurity professionals.

For CM to become a reality for any agency, it must meet the measures and expectations defined in the National Institute of Standards and Technology (NIST) Special Publication (SP) 800-137, Information

Security Continuous Monitoring for Federal Information Systems and Organizations. "Continuous monitoring has evolved as a best practice for managing risk on an ongoing basis" (SANS Institute, 2016); it is an instrument that supports effective, continual, and recurring RM assurances. For any agency to indeed espouse it has attained full CM compliance, it must coordinate all the described major elements as found in NIST SP 800-137.

CM is not just the passive visibility pieces but also includes the active efforts of vulnerability scanning, threat alert, reduction, mitigation, or elimination of a dynamic Information Technology (IT) environment. The Department of Homeland Security (DHS) has couched its approach to CM more holistically. Their program to protect government networks is more aptly called: "Continuous Diagnostics and Monitoring" or CDM and includes a need to react to an active network attacker. "The ability to make IT networks, end-points and applications visible; to identify malicious activity; and, to respond [emphasis added] immediately is critical to defending information systems and networks" (Sann, 2016).

Another description of CM can be found in NIST's CAESARS Framework Extension: An Enterprise Continuous Monitoring Technical Reference Model (Second Draft). It defines its essential characteristics within the concept of "Continuous Security Monitoring." It is described as a "...risk management approach to Cybersecurity that maintains a picture of an organization's security posture, provides visibility into assets, leverages the use of automated data feeds, monitors the effectiveness of security controls, and enables prioritization of remedies" (NIST, 2012); it must demonstrate visibility, data feeds, measures of effectiveness and allow for solutions. It provides another description of what should be presented to ensure full CM designation under the NIST standard.

The government's Federal Risk and Authorization Management Program (Fed-RAMP) has defined similar CM goals. These objectives are all key outcomes of a successful CM implementation. Its "... goal[s]...[are] to provide: (i) operational visibility; (ii) annual self-attestation on security control implementations; (iii) managed change control; (iv) and attendance to incident response duties," (GSA, 2012). While not explicit to NIST SP 800-37, these objectives are well-aligned with the desires of an effective and complete solution.

RMF creates the structure and documentation needs of CM; CM represents the specific implementation and oversight of Information Security (IS) within an IT environment. It supports the general activity of RM within an agency. (See Figure 1 below). The RMF "... describes a disciplined and structured process that integrates information security and risk management activities into the system development life cycle" (NIST-B, 2011). RMF is the structure that both describes and relies upon CM as its risk oversight and effective mechanism between IS and RM.

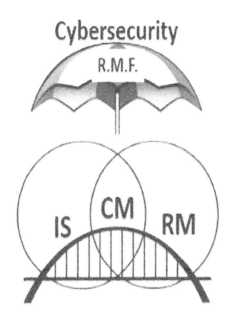

Figure 1. CM "bridges" Information Security and Risk Management

This article provides a conceptual framework to address how an agency would identify a correct CM solution through NIST SP 800-137. It discusses the additional need to align component requirements with the

"11 Security Automation Domains" necessary to implement true CM. (See Figure 2 below). It is through the complete implementation and

Figure 2. The 11 Security Automation Domains (NIST, 2011)

integration with the other described components—See Figure 3 below—that an organization can correctly state it has achieved CM.

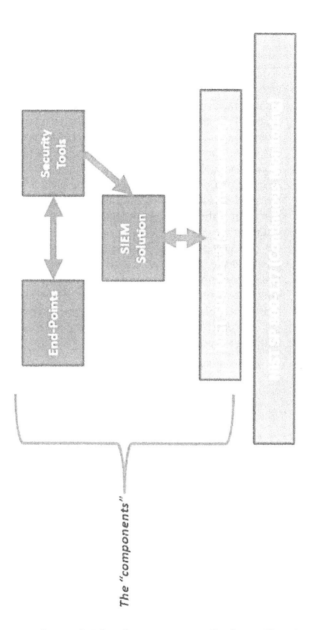

Figure 3. The "Components" of an Effective Continuous Monitoring

Continuous Monitoring – First Generation

For CM to be effective and genuine, it must align end-point visibility with security monitoring tools. This includes security monitoring tools with connectivity to "end-points" such as laptops, desktops, servers, routers, firewalls, etc. Additionally, these must work with a highly integrated Security Information and Event Management (SIEM) device. The other "component" is a clear linkage between the end-points, security monitoring tools, and the SIEM appliance, working with the *Security Automation Domains* (See Figure 2). These would include, for example, the areas of malware detection, asset, and event management. CM must first address these composite components to create a "First Generation" instantiation.

A SIEM appliance provides the central core data processing capabilities to effectively coordinate all the inputs and outputs from across the IT enterprise. It manages the data integration and interpretation of all CM components. Moreover, it provides the necessary visibility and intelligence for an operational incident response capability.

In describing a *First Generation* implementation, the following arithmetic expression is offered:

$$\text{END-POINTS}_{\text{VISIBILITY}} + \text{SECURITY TOOLS}_{\text{MONITORING}} + \text{SECURITY CONTROLS}_{\text{ALIGNMENT}} \rightarrow \text{(INPUT) SIEM SOLUTION} \rightarrow 11 \text{ SECURITY AUTOMATION DOMAINS}_{\text{COMPARISON}} \rightarrow \text{(OUTPUT) [VISIBILITY + ANALYSIS + ALERTS]} = \text{CM}_{\text{FIRST GEN}}$$

An Arithmetic Expression for First-Generation Continuous Monitoring

End-point devices must be persistently visible to the applicable security devices. Together, these parts must align with the respective security controls described in NIST SP 800-53. The selected SIEM tool must accept these inputs and analyze them against defined security policy settings, recurring vulnerability scans, signature-based threats, and heuristic/activity-based analyses to ensure the environment's security posture. The SIEM outputs must support the IT environment's further visibility, conduct, and disseminate vital intelligence, and mindful leadership to any ongoing or imminent dangers. The expression above is designed to provide a conceptual representation of the cybersecurity professional attempting to ascertain effective CM implementation or develop a complete CM answer for an agency or corporation.

Additionally, the SIEM must distribute data feeds in near-real-time to analysts and critical leaders. It provides for multi-level "dashboard" data streams, and issues alert based upon prescribed policy settings. Once these base, First Generation functionalities are consistently aligning with the Security Automation Domains, then an organization or corporation can definitively express it meets the requirements of CM.

End-Points

It is necessary to identify hardware and software configuration items that must be known and constantly traceable before implementing CM within an enterprise IT environment. End-point visibility is not the hardware devices but the hardware device's baseline software on the network.

Configuration Management is also a foundational requirement for any organization's security posture. Soundly implemented Configuration Management must be the basis of any complete CM implementation. At the beginning of any IS effort, cyber-professionals must know the current "as-is" hardware and software component state within the enterprise. End-points must be protected and monitored because they are the most valuable target for would-be hackers and cyber-thieves.

Configuration Management provides the baseline that establishes a means to identify potential compromise between the enterprise's end-points and the requisite security tools. "Organizations with a robust and effective [Configuration Management] process need to consider information security implications concerning the development and operation of information systems including hardware, software, applications, and documentation" (NIST-A, 2011).

The RMF requires the categorization of systems and data as high, moderate, or low regarding risk. The Federal Information Processing Standards (FIPS) Publication 199 methodology is typically used to establish the federal government's data sensitivity levels. FIPS 199 aids the cybersecurity professional in determining data protection standards of both end-points and the data stored in these respective parts. For example, a system that collects and retains sensitive data, such as financial information, requires a higher security level. End-points must be recognized as repositories of highly valued data to cyber-threats.

Further, cyber-security professionals must be constantly aware of the "...administrative and technological costs of offering a high degree of protection for all federal systems..." (Ross, Katzke, & Toth, 2005). This is not a matter of recognizing the physical end-point alone, but the value and associated costs of the virtual data stored, monitored, and protected continually. FIPS 199 helps system owners determine whether a higher level of protection is warranted, with higher associated costs, based upon an overall FIPS 199 evaluation.

Security Tools

Security monitoring tools must identify in near-real-time an active threat. Examples include anti-virus or anti-malware applications used to monitor network and end-point activities. Products like McAfee and Symantec provide enterprise capabilities that help to identify and reduce threats.

Other security tools would address in whole or part the remaining NIST Security Automation Domains. These would include, for example, tools to provide asset visibility, vulnerability detection, patch management updates, etc. However, it is also critical to recognize that even the best current security tools cannot defend against all attacks. New malware or zero-day attacks pose continual challenges to the cybersecurity workforce.

For example, DHS's EINSTEIN system would not have stopped the 2015 Office of Personnel Management breach. Even DHS's latest iteration of EINSTEIN, EINSTEIN 3, an advanced network monitoring and response system designed to protect federal governments' networks, would not have stopped that attack. "…EINSTEIN 3 would not have been able to catch a threat that [had] no known footprints, according to multiple industry experts" (Sternstein, 2015).

Not until there are a much higher integration and availability of cross-cutting intelligence and more capable security tools can any single security tool ever be entirely useful. The need for multiple security monitoring tools that provide "defense in depth" may be a better protective strategy. However, with various tools monitoring the same Security Automation Domains, such an approach will undoubtedly increase the costs of maintaining a secure agency or corporate IT environment. A determination of Return on Investment (ROI) balanced against a well-defined threat risk scoring approach is further needed at all federal and corporate IT workspace levels.

Security Controls

"Organizations are required to adequately mitigate the risk arising from the use of information and information systems in the execution of missions and business functions" (NIST, 2013). This is accomplished by selecting and implementing NIST SP 800-53, Revision 4, described security controls. (See Figure 4 below). They are organized into eighteen families to address sub-set security areas such as access control, physical security, incident response, etc. The use of these controls is typically tailored to the respective system owner's security categorization relying upon FIPS 199 categorization standards. A higher security categorization requires the greater implementation of these controls.

ID	FAMILY	ID	FAMILY
AC	Access Control	MP	Media Protection
AT	Awareness and Training	PE	Physical and Environmental Protection
AU	Audit and Accountability	PL	Planning
CA	Security Assessment and Authorization	PS	Personnel Security
CM	Configuration Management	RA	Risk Assessment
CP	Contingency Planning	SA	System and Services Acquisition
IA	Identification and Authentication	SC	System and Communications Protection
IR	Incident Response	SI	System and Information Integrity
MA	Maintenance	PM	Program Management

Figure 4. Security Control Identifiers and Family Names (NIST, 2013)

Security Information and Event Management (SIEM) Solutions

The SIEM tool plays a pivotal role in any viable "First Generation" implementation. Based on NIST and DHS guidance, a capable SIEM appliance must provide the following functionalities:

- "Aggregate data from "across a diverse set" of security tool sources;
- Analyze the multi-source data;
- Engage in explorations of data based on changing needs
- Make quantitative use of data for security (not just reporting) purposes, including the development and use of risk scores; and

- Maintain actionable awareness of the changing security situation on a real-time basis" (Levinson, 2011).

"Effectiveness is further enhanced when the output is formatted to provide information that is specific, measurable, actionable, relevant, and timely" (NIST, 2011). The SIEM device is the vital core of a full solution that collects, analyzes, and alerts the cyber-professional of potential and actual dangers in their environment.

Several major SIEM solutions can effectively meet the requirements of NIST SP 800-137. They include products, for example, IBM® Security, Splunk®, and Hewlett Packard's® ArcSight® products.

For example, Logrhythm ® was highly rated in the 2014 SIEM evaluation. Logrhythm® provided network event monitoring and alerts of potential security compromises. Implementing an enterprise-grade SIEM solution is necessary to meet growing cybersecurity requirements for auditing security logs and capabilities to respond to cyber-incidents. SIEM products will continue to play a critical and evolving role in the demands for "...increased security and rapid response to events throughout the network" (McAfee® Foundstone Professional Services®, 2013). Improvements and upgrades of SIEM tools are critical to providing a more highly responsive capability for future generations of these appliances in the marketplace.

Next Generations

Future generations of CM would include specific expanded capabilities and functionalities of the SIEM device. These second generation and beyond evolutions would be more effective solutions in future dynamic and hostile network environments. Such advancements might also include increased access to a greater pool of threat database signature repositories or more expansive heuristics to identify functional anomalies within a target network.

Another futuristic capability might include the use of Artificial Intelligence (AI). Improved SIEM capabilities with AI augmentation would further enhance human threat analysis and provide for more automated responsiveness. "The concept of predictive analysis involves using statistical methods and decision tools that analyze current and historical data to make predictions about future events..." (SANS Institute). The next generation would boost human response times and abilities to defend against attacks in a matter of milli-seconds vice hours.

Finally, in describing the next generations of CM, it is not only imperative to expand data, informational, and intelligence inputs for new and more capable SIEM products, but that input and corresponding data sets must also be thoroughly vetted for completeness and accuracy. Increased access to signature and heuristic activity-based analysis databases would provide a more significant risk reduction. More substantial support from private industry and the Intelligence Community would also be significant improvements for Agencies that are continually struggling against a more-capable and better-resourced threat.

CM will not be a reality until vendors and agencies can integrate the right people, processes, and technologies. "Security needs to be positioned as an enabler of the organization—it must take its place alongside human resources, financial resources, sound business processes and strategies, information technology, and intellectual capital as the elements of success for accomplishing the mission" (Caralli, 2004). CM is not just a technical solution. It requires capable organizations with trained personnel, creating effective policies and procedures with the requisite technologies to stay ahead of cyberspace's growing threats.

Figure 6 below provides a graphic depiction of what CM components are needed to create a holistic NIST SP 800-137-compliant solution; this demonstrates the First-Generation representation. Numerous vendors describe that they have the "holy grail" solution. Still, until they can prove they meet this description in total, it is unlikely they have a complete implementation of a complete CM solution yet.

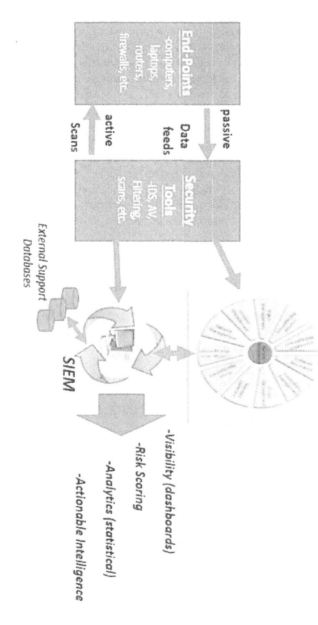

First Generation Continuous Monitoring

References

Balakrishnan, B. (2015, October 6). *Insider Threat Mitigation Guidance*. Retrieved from SANS Institute Infosec Reading Room: https://www.sans.org/reading-room/whitepapers/monitoring/insider-threat-mitigation-guidance-36307

Caralli, R. A. (2004, December). *Managing Enterprise Security (CMU/SEI-2004-TN-046)*. Retrieved from Software Engineering Institute: http://www.sei.cmu.edu/reports/04tn046.pdf

Committee on National Security Systems. (2010, April 26). *National Information Assurance (IA) Glossary*. Retrieved from National Counterintelligence & Security Center: http://www.ncsc.gov/nittf/docs/CNSSI-4009_National_Information_Assurance.pdf

Department of Defense. (2014, March 12). *DOD Instructions 8510.01: Risk Management Framework (RMF) for DoD Information Technology (IT)*. Retrieved from Defense Technical Information Center (DTIC): http://www.dtic.mil/whs/directives/corres/pdf/851001_2014.pdf

GSA. (2012, January 27). *Continuous Monitoring Strategy & Guide, v1.1*. Retrieved from General Services Administration: http://www.gsa.gov/graphics/staffoffices/Continuous_Monitoring_Strategy_Guide_072712.pdf

Joint Medical Logistics Functional Development Center. (2015). JMLFDC Continuous Monitoring Strategy Plan and Procedure. Ft Detrick, MD.

Kavanagh, K. M., Nicolett, M., & Rochford, O. (2014, June 25). *Magic Quadrant for Security Information and Event Management*. Retrieved from Gartner: http://www.gartner.com/technology/reprints.do?id=1-1W8AO4W&ct=140627&st=sb&mkt_tok=3RkMMJWWfF9wsRolsqrJcO%2FhmjTEU5z17u8lWa%2B0gYkz2EFye%2BLIHETpodcMTcVkNb%2FYDBceEJhqyQJxPr3FKdANz8JpRhngAA%3D%3D

Kolenko, M. M. (2016, February 18). *SPECIAL-The Human Element of Cybersecurity*. Retrieved from Homeland Security Today.US: http://www.hstoday.us/briefings/industry-news/single-article/special-the-human-element-of-cybersecurity/54008efd46e93863f54db0f7352dde2c.html

Levinson, B. (2011, October). *Federal Cybersecurity Best Practices Study: Information Security Continuous Monitoring.* Retrieved from Center for Regulatory Effectiveness: http://www.thecre.com/fisma/wp-content/uploads/2011/10/Federal-Cybersecurity-Best-Practice.ISCM_2.pdf

McAfee® Foundstone® Professional Services. (2013). *McAfee.* Retrieved from White Paper: Creating and Maintaining a SOC: http://www.mcafee.com/us/resources/white-papers/foundstone/wp-creating-maintaining-soc.pdf

NIST. (2011-A, August). *NIST SP 800-128: Guide for Security-Focused Configuration Management of Information Systems.* Retrieved from NIST Computer Security Resource Center: http://csrc.nist.gov/publications/nistpubs/800-128/sp800_128.pdf

NIST. (2011-B, September). *Special Publication 800-137: Information Security Continuous Monitoring (ISCM) for Federal Information Systems and Organizations.* Retrieved from NIST Computer Security Resource Center: http://csrc.nist.gov/publications/nistpubs/800-137/SP800-137-Final.pdf

NIST. (2012, January). *NIST Interagency Report 7756: CAESARS Framework Extension: An Enterprise Continuous Monitoring Technical Reference Model (Second Draft).* Retrieved from NIST Computer Resource Security Center: http://csrc.nist.gov/publications/drafts/nistir-7756/Draft-NISTIR-7756_second-public-draft.pdf

NIST. (2013, April). *NIST SP 800-53, Rev 4: Security and Privacy Controls for Federal Information Systems.* Retrieved from NIST: http://nvlpubs.nist.gov/nistpubs/SpecialPublications/NIST.SP.800-53r4.pdf

Ross, R., Katzke, S., & Toth, P. (2005, October 17). *The New FISMA Standards and Guidelines Changing the Dynamic of Information Security for the Federal Government.* Retrieved from Information Technology Promotion Agency of Japan: https://www.ipa.go.jp/files/000015362.pdf

Sann, W. (2016, January 8). *The Key Missing Piece of Your Cyber Strategy? Visibility.* Retrieved from Nextgov: http://www.nextgov.com/technology-news/tech-insider/2016/01/key-missing-element-your-cyber-strategy-visibility/124974/

SANS Institute. (2016, March 6). *Beyond Continuous Monitoring: Threat Modeling for Real-time Response.* Retrieved from SANS Institute: http://www.sans.org/reading-room/whitepapers/analyst/continuous-monitoring-threat-modeling-real-time-response-35185

Sternstein, A. (2015, January 6). *OPM Hackers Skirted Cutting-Edge Intrusion Detection System, Official Says.* Retrieved from Nextgov: http://www.nextgov.com/cybersecurity/2015/06/opm-hackers-skirted-cutting-edge-interior-intrusion-detection-official-says/114649/

APPENDIX D – MANAGING THE LIFECYCLE OF A POAM

Intelligence Cycle Approach for the POAM Lifecycle

This section is designed to provide a structure for anyone developing a POAM for their company or agency. It describes how to easily approach the POAM development process and formulate and track POAMs during their lifecycle. We suggest using the US Intelligence Community's *Intelligence Lifecycle* as a guide to address POAM's from "cradle-to-grave." The process has been slightly modified to provide a more pertinent description for POAM creation. Still, we have found this model useful for the novice through professional cybersecurity or IT specialist that regularly works in this arena.

This includes the following six stages:

1. **IDENTIFY** Those controls that time, technology, or cost cannot be met to satisfy the unimplemented control.

2. **RESEARCH:** You now have decided the control is not going to meet your immediate CMMC needs. The typical initial milestone is to conduct some form of research or market survey of available solutions. This will include:

    - **The kind or type of solution.** Either as a person (e.g., additional expertise), process (e.g., what established workflow can provide a repeatable solution), or technology (e.g., what hardware/software solution fixes all or part of the control.
    - **How the federal government wants it implemented?** For example, are hard tokens required, or can the company use soft token solutions to address 2FA?
    - **Internal challenges.** What does the company face overall with people, process, or technology perspectives specific to the control?

3. **RECOMMEND:** At this phase, all research and analysis has been done and presumably well-documented. Typically, the cybersecurity team or business IT team will formulate recommended solutions to the System Owner, i.e., the business decision-makers such as the Chief Information or Operations Officer. The recommendations must be technically feasible, but cost and resources should be part of any recommendation.

4. **DECIDE:** At this point, company decision-makers not only approve of the approach to correct the security shortfall but have agreed to resource requirements to authorize the expenditures of funds and efforts.

5. **IMPLEMENT:** Finally, the solution is implemented, and the POAM is updated for closure. This should be reported to the Contract Office or its representative regularly.

6. **CONTINUAL IMPROVEMENT.** Like any process, it should be regularly reviewed and updated accurately to the company or organization's needs and capabilities. This could include better templates, additional staffing, or more regular updates to management to ensure both a thorough but supportive understanding of how cybersecurity meets the business's needs and mission.

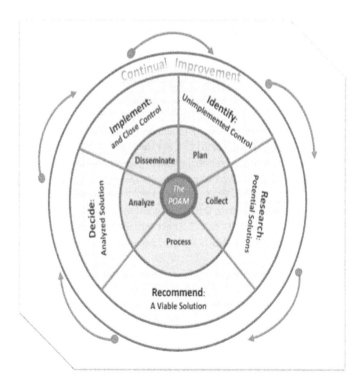

The POAM Lifecycle

We begin in the "Identify" section of the lifecycle process above. At this stage, several things may occur. The business owner or IT staff recognizes that the security control is not or cannot be immediately met, or they employ an automated security tool, such as ACAS® or Nessus®, that identifies securities vulnerabilities within the IS. This could also include findings such as the default password, like "password," which has not been changed on an internal switch or router. It could also include updated security patching that has not occurred; some automated applications will not only identify but recommend courses of action to mitigate or fix a security finding. Always try to leverage those as soon as possible to secure your IT environment.

Also, assumed in this stage is the act of documenting findings. The finding should be placed in a POAM template as the business moves through the lifecycle. This could be done using documents created in Word®, for example, but recommend using a spreadsheet program that allows the easier filtering and management of the POAM. Spreadsheets afford greater flexibility during the "heavy lift" portion of formulating all POAMs not intended to be fixed immediately because of technical shortfalls. This would include not having in-house technical expertise, such as setting up Two Factor Authentication (2FA) or current company financial limitations; this would most likely be reasonable when the costs are currently prohibitive to implement specific control.

The "research" phase includes technical analysis, Internet searches, market research, etc., regarding viable solutions to address the security control not being "compliant." This activity is typically part of an initial milestone established in the POAM. It may be added in the POAM and could be, for example: "Conduct initial market research of candidate systems that can provide an affordable Two Factor Authentication (2FA) solution to meet security control 3.X.X." Another example might be: "The cybersecurity section will identify at least two candidate Data at Rest (DAR) solutions to protect the company's corporate and CUI data." These initial milestones are a normal part of any initial milestones that clearly describe reasonable actions to address non-compliant controls.

Another part of any milestone establishment action is to identify when a milestone is expected to be complete. Typically, milestones are done for 30 days, but if such an activity's complexity requires additional time, ensure the company has identified reasonable periods with actual dates of *expected* completion. Never use undefined milestones such as "next version update" or "Calendar Year 2020 in Quarter 4." Real times are mandatory to manage findings supported by, for example, automated workflow or tracking applications the company may acquire in the future to enhance its cybersecurity risk management program.

At the "recommendation" phase, this is the time when the prior research has resulted in at least one solution, be it additional skilled personnel (people), enhanced company policies that manage the security control better (process), or a device that solves the control in part or total (technology). This should be part of this phase and be part of the POAM template as a milestone with the expected completion date.

At the "decide" phase, company or agency decision-makers should approve a recommended solution. That decision should be documented in a configuration change tracking document, configuration management decision memorandum, or in the POAM itself. This should include approved resources, but most importantly, any funding decision should be acted upon as quickly as possible. While many of these suggestions may seem necessary, it is often overlooked to document the decision so future personnel and management can understand how the solution was determined.

The "implementation" phase may become the most difficult. A leader should be designated to coordinate the specific activity to meet the control— it may not necessarily be a technical solution. Still, it may also include, for example, a documentation development activity that creates a process to manage the POAM.

Implementation should also include primary programmatic considerations. This should consist of performance, schedule, cost, and risk:

- Performance: consider what success the solution is attempting to address. Will it send email alerts to users? Will the system shutdown automatically once an intrusion is confirmed in the corporate network? Will the Incident Response Plan include notifications to law enforcement? Performance is always an effective and measurable means to ensure that the solution will address the POAM/security control shortfall. Always try to measure performance specific to the actual control that is being met.

- Schedule: Devise a plan based upon the developed milestones that are reasonable and not unrealistic. As soon as a deviation becomes apparent, ensure that the POAM template is updated and approved by management. This should be a senior management representative with the authority to provide extensions to the current plan. This could include, for example, a Senior IT Manager, Chief Information Security Officer, or Chief Operating Officer.

- Cost: While it is assumed that all funding has been provided early in the process, always ensure contingencies are in place to request additional funding. It is common in most IT programs to maintain a 15-20% funding reserve for emergencies. Otherwise, the Project Manager or lead will have to re-justify to management for additional funding late in the cycle's implementation portion.

- Risk: This is not the risk identified, for example, by the review of security controls or automated scans of the system. This risk is specific to the program's success in accomplishing its goal to close the security finding. Risk should always focus on the performance, cost, and schedule risks as significant concerns. Consider creating a risk matrix or risk log to help during the implementation phase.

Finally, ensure that the company can satisfactorily implement its solution close the control, and notify the Contract Office of the completion. Typically, updates and notifications should occur at least once a quarter, but more often is appropriate for more highly impactful controls. Two-factor authentication and automated auditing, for example, are best updated as quickly as possible. This not only secures the company's network and IT environment but builds confidence with the government that security requirements are being met.

A final area to consider in terms of best-practices within cybersecurity, and more specifically, in developing complete POAMs, is the area of **continual improvement**. Leveraging the legacy Intelligence Lifecycle process should be an ongoing model for IT and cybersecurity specialists to emulate. Those supporting this process should always be prepared to make changes or modifications that better represent the system's state and readiness with its listing of POAMs. The Intelligence Lifecycle provides the ideal model for a business to follow and implement to meet its POAM responsibilities within the CMMC.

ABOUT THE AUTHOR

Mr. Russo is a Chief Data Scientist supporting the DOD with advanced data analytics and technical expertise to identify Tactics, Techniques, and Procedures posed by global cyber-threats. He is a former Senior Information Security Engineer within the Department of Defense's (DOD) F-35 Joint Strike Fighter program. He has an extensive background in cybersecurity and is an expert in the Risk Management Framework (RMF) and DOD Instruction 8510, which implements RMF throughout the DOD and the federal government. He holds both a Certified Information Systems Security Professional (CISSP) certification and a CISSP in information security architecture (ISSAP). He has a 2017 certificate as a Chief Information Security Officer (CISO) from the National Defense University, Washington, DC. He retired from the US Army in 2012 as a Senior Intelligence Officer.

He is the former CISO at the Department of Education, wherein 2016; he led the effort to close over 95% of the outstanding US Congressional and Inspector General cybersecurity shortfall weaknesses spanning as far back as five years.

In 2011, Mr. Russo was certified by the Office of Personnel Management as a graduate of the Senior Executive Service Candidate program.

Mr. Russo was the first-ever Program Executive Officer (PEO)/Senior Program Manager in the Office of Intelligence & Analysis at Headquarters, Department of Homeland Security (DHS), Washington, DC. Mr. Russo was responsible for the development and deployment of secure Information and Intelligence support systems for OI&A to include software applications and systems to enhance the DHS mission. He was responsible for the program management development lifecycle during his tenure at DHS.

He holds a Master of Science from the National Defense University in Government Information Leadership with a concentration in Cybersecurity and a Bachelor of Arts in Political Science with a minor in Russian Studies from Lehigh University. He holds Level III Defense Acquisition certification in Program Management, Information Technology, and Systems Engineering. He has been a member of the DOD Acquisition Corps since 2001.

Copyright 2021, Cybersentinel, LLC, All Rights Reserved
Washington, DC ∞ Tucson, AZ

Made in the USA
Monee, IL
21 April 2022